D1173110

MUDDY BOOTS LEADERSHIP

*Real-Life Stories and Personal Examples of Good,
Bad, and Unexpected Results*

by
John Chapman

STACKPOLE BOOKS

0 11557 00166 2

Copyright © 2006 by Stackpole Books

Published by
STACKPOLE BOOKS
5067 Ritter Road
Mechanicsburg, PA 17055
www.stackpolebooks.com

All rights reserved, including the right to reproduce this book or portions thereof in any form or by any means, electronic or mechanical, including photocopying, recording, or by any information storage and retrieval system, without permission in writing from the publisher. All inquiries should be addressed to Stackpole Books at the above address.

Cover design by Wendy Reynolds

Printed in the United States of America

10 9 8 7 6 5

Library of Congress Cataloging-in Publication Data
Chapman, John (John E.)
  Muddy boots leadership : real life stories and personal examples of good, bad, and unexpected results / by John Chapman.
     p. cm.
  Includes index.
  ISBN 0-8117-0166-2 (alk. paper)
  1. Leadership. 2. Command of troops. I. Title.

UB210.C482 2006
355.3'3041—dc22

2006002776

ISBN 978-0-8117-0166-2

Table of Contents

PROFESSIONAL COMPETENCE

SOLDIERS

Foreword

Author John Chapman, a superb observer and chronicler of leadership events, now shares in this book his observations and lessons learned about this essential military art. Today's unit-level military leaders can learn much from their predecessors in what works and what doesn't. In this book, Chapman covers just about every area of leadership and leadership interaction with followers, which in turn produces a large number of stories and vignettes servicemen will immediately recognize.

Leadership has many purposes—to build effective organizations, to successfully complete dangerous tasks in high-risk environments, and to mold teams that operate like winning sports teams.

For their part, the military services, as institutions, have a fairly common understanding of leadership. In no other profession is lack of sound leadership more potentially disastrous than in the armed forces. At the most basic level, military leaders are selected for their proven ability to do two things: (a) accomplish the *mission,* and (2) take care of their *people*—in that priority!

The primary task of any military organization is to perform its mission. This is paramount. As a leader, your primary responsibility is to lead people to carry out the unit's mission successfully.

People perform the mission. They are the heart of any organization, and without their support the unit will fail in its mission. The successful leader is the one fitted by force of ideas, character, genius, and strength of will to arouse, excite, and direct individuals in their performance of duties necessary for the accomplishment of the mission.

Most leaders must, by the nature of their positions, also be managers. But there is a difference. *Leadership* is the art of influencing and directing people to accomplish the mission. *Management* is the manner in which both human and material resources are applied to achieve objectives. In essence, the leader leads people and manages assets.

All of the military services have relatively similar definitions of the ideal traits and characteristics of a leader. In the Army, these go by the acronym L-D-R-S-H-I-P, which include:

—*Loyalty* is to bear true faith and allegiance to the U.S. Constitution, the Army, your unit, and your fellow soldiers.

—*Duty* means fulfilling your professional obligations to do something, and doing it to the highest standard.

—*Respect* is to treat people as they should be treated and as you would want to be treated.

—*Selfless Service* means to put the welfare of the nation, the Army, and your subordinates before your own welfare or desires or pleasures.

—*Honor* is to behave with human dignity, to be honest, to fulfill a commitment, to keep a promise.

—*Integrity* is doing what's right, legally and morally.

—*Personal Courage* is to perform your duty in the face of fear, danger, or adversity (physical or moral).

Complementing these bedrock values are two leadership characteristics essential for professional success: *Teamwork* and

Discipline. Military units cannot operate in peace or war without these two characteristics.

The Air Force uses a similar list of leader characteristics, but adds:

—*Decisiveness,* the willingness to act, to take timely and affirmative decisions.

—*Energy,* an enthusiasm, drive, and aggressiveness to take the initiative.

All the services agree that the leadership principles "know yourself, know your job, and set the example" are imperatives for leadership.

As you read through this book, you will find numerous examples of leader actions and decisions—some are humorous, some tragic. Many are examples of good leadership, others of not so good leadership, and some actions that caused quite unexpected results. Use these examples as a guide to your future actions, regardless of whether you are a commissioned officer, a warrant officer, a noncommissioned officer, or a soldier, airman, sailor, marine, or a civilian who aspires to leadership.

Acknowledgment

This document is the result of many fine soldiers with whom I have been privileged to serve. They include Colonels Ronald Robinson and John Spears; Lt. Col. Bruce Shabaz; Captains Joel Bagnal, Randal Flood, Jerry Stephens, Paul Shelton, and Randy West; 1st Sgt. Carr; Sergeants First Class Dennis Reilly, James Lyons, and James McGrath; Drill Sergeant Antrupp; Specialist Richard Richardson; and many others.

Regrettably, some of these lessons learned must be attributed to the weak, lazy, or excruciatingly bad leaders with and under whom I have unfortunately had to suffer. They remain nameless but not forgotten.

John E. Chapman
Spring 2006

LEADERSHIP

Leadership is a potent combination of strategy and character.
But if you must be without one, be without the strategy.

—GEN. H. NORMAN SCHWARZKOPF

LEADERSHIP AGREEMENT

Disagreement is not disloyalty before the decision is made. Soldiers have a professional obligation to present honest opinions, assessments and disagreements during the decision process. After the boss had made a decision, there is no room for dissent. It is now your decision too.

"I don't want any yes-men around me. I want everybody to tell me the truth, even if it costs them their jobs."

—SAMUEL GOLDWYN

CHECKING

Trust but verify. Show up at the least-expected time and place to check on your troops' performance and how they are being treated, particularly if they are on detail with another command.

"Trust but verify."

—RONALD REAGAN

Start with the smallest, least-visible tasking. You will be the first leader to ever check those soldiers.

CHAIRBOUND IGNORANCE

Get out of your office! If you remain glued to your comfortable and isolated chair, you will know little and be little.

Your precious reports and forms and briefings will tell you only what you ask for, not what you need to know. This two-dimensional illusion is not true. As does art, it only imitates reality.

Get out of your office. Walk around. Ask questions. Be on patrol within your unit. The worse the weather, the later the hour, the darker the night, the more important it is to get out to see and *be seen.*

The worse the weather, the later the hour, the darker the night, the more important it is to get out to see and be seen.

COMMON SENSE

If it sounds like a dumb thing and it looks like a dumb thing, maybe it is a dumb thing.

Your soldiers are not West Point graduates. They make decisions based on a little bit of education and a lot of common sense. If you make a foolish decision based on a lot of education and very little common sense, you will become a legend.

"Common sense to an uncommon degree is what the world calls wisdom."
—SAMUEL TAYLOR COLERIDGE

PERSONAL COMMITMENT

Leslie D. Weatherhead on comradeship . . .

When a solider was injured and could not get back to safety, his buddy went out to get him, against his officer's orders. He returned mortally wounded and his friend, whom he had carried back, was dead.

The officer was angry. "I told you not to go," he said. "Now I've lost both of you. It was not worth it." The dying man replied, "But it was, sir, because when I got to him he said, 'Jim, I knew you'd come.'"

Source: *"An anthology of letters, reading and notes"* assembled by two soldiers in the Army War College and published by Brig. Gen. Herbert J. Lloyd, ADCS, 2nd Infantry Division, 13 Nov 1990

Real Life

The 1-3 Cav mess sergeant was furious. His cooks had failed to properly inventory the chow pick-up, and now they were short. Someone would have to choke down the hated MREs again, instead of the first hot food served to the squadron in several exhausting days.

His voice hot with anger, he snapped off the words, "All the hot chow goes forward. You, me and the rest of headquarters company are having MREs."

The soldiers shivering in foxholes eight kilometers to his front never knew of this decision. His rater and senior rater (both within headquarters company) certainly knew by mealtime, and didn't appreciate it. Why did he do it?

Real Life

The commander asked the first sergeant if the [charity] Christmas food basket request was complete. The senior NCO casually replied, "The platoon sergeants did not care enough to submit any names; why should I?"

The first sergeant lost ground that day. His commitment to soldiers and doing the right thing was always suspect after that.

Everything in life is a graded event.

COURTESY
Don't mistake courtesy for weakness; more importantly, don't allow your soldiers to make that mistake about you.

COMMENDATIONS

"Admonish your friends in private; praise them in public."

—PUBLILIUS SYRUS, 50 BC

Ass-chewing done in private, commendations done in public. This was good advice 2,000 years ago, good leadership today.

CREDIBILITY

Your credibility with soldiers, and the trust it engenders, grows from their perception of your professional competence and personal ethics. Soldiers hear what you tell them but they *believe what they see.*

If you correct a soldier for a uniform violation, your uniform must be right. If you admonish a soldier for poorly shined boots then yours must be shined, and today should not be the first time you shined them. To effectively encourage a soldier to try harder on the physical fitness test, to hang-tough and squeeze out those last two push-ups, he can never see you quit with time remaining, no matter what your score is.

Everything in life is a graded event.

"The first thing a young officer must do when he joins the Army is to fight a battle, and that battle is for the hearts of his men. If he wins that battle and subsequent similar ones, his men will follow him anywhere; if he loses it, he will never do any real good."

—FIELD MARSHAL BERNARD L. MONTGOMERY

CREDIT & BLAME

When something goes wrong, ensure that your instructions were understood. If they were not, the blame is yours. If you were understood, look for someone to teach rather than blame.

A common but wise truism: fix the problem, not the blame.

UNIT BONDING

Shared experience builds bonding. The more intense the experience, the stronger the bond.

Great suffering equals strong bonding.

Bonding is built on the group and individual acceptance that each person is a valued part of the team and has a secure place in the organization. Intense, battle-focused training forces' reliance on one another, bonds new groups, and reinforces existing ones.

PERSONAL GROWTH

"We find comfort among those who agree with us—growth among those who don't."

—FRANK A. CLARK

You don't know all the answers. Acting as though you do discourages thoughtful discussion and honest disagreement from those around you. Discussion and disagreement are the great fertilizers of personal growth.

The self-inflicted isolation of the "know-it-all" slows his personal and professional development. Ironically, his myopic actions become part of the developmental discussion of his peers. They grow at his expense.

HONESTY WITH OTHERS

"The man who is brutally honest enjoys the brutality quite as much as the honesty. Possibly more."

—RICHARD J. NEEDHAM

A reputation for honesty is built over a lifetime and lost in a moment. Be honest. Don't be brutal, but *be honest.*

Real Life

The colonel and his company commanders evaluated their National Guard sister unit's annual training. Initial performance was weak and improved little.

Each evening the active duty officers briefed their battalion commander on the day's training objectives and the sister unit's poor performance. The colonel ended these meetings with an angry lecture that left no doubt of his poor opinion of the Guard unit and its leaders.

Both the active duty and the Guard unit's brigade commanders attended the final out brief. The colonel's evaluation of the National Guard Battalion changed to meet what he thought was their political expectation. The evaluated unit commander received a glowing assessment and a framed certificate of achievement from the malleable active-duty battalion commander.

Each accolade the active duty colonel heaped upon his counterpart further damaged his already tarnished reputation for honesty. Perhaps he didn't consider the fact that many of his subordinates in the audience knew the truth, or maybe he just didn't care.

FIRST IMPRESSIONS

First impressions are not always accurate or fair. They are, however, powerful and long lasting.

The less known about you, the more important the first impression is. The more known, the harder it is to change your reputation, regardless of the first impression, good or bad.

"If you want to succeed, you'd better look as if you mean business."

—JEANNE HOLM

Real Life

During a pause in his platoon's live fire exercise, the young lieutenant dismounted his Bradley fighting vehicle. Although burdened with his combat equipment, he hurried toward the range tower. He passed by his battalion and brigade commanders, who were observing the training. He instinctively saluted and rendered the greeting he demanded of his soldiers, "Shoot 'em in the face, Sir!"

As the young officer walked away, the brigade commander commented, "I like that man's attitude! What is his name?"

The lieutenant had been in the unit only a short time, yet his first impression with the brigade commander was powerful and positive.

Real Life

The lieutenant arrived while his new unit was involved in a large field training exercise. He was quickly transported to the training site, carrying both of the required duffel bags and his rucksack through the oppressive heat of Fort Hood in July. He reported to the battalion executive officer (XO), his new senior rater. The XO told him to report to the supply and personnel section and then return.

The new man desperately carried his gear up and down the dusty hills for an hour. He sadly returned to reluctantly report failure to his new senior rater, on his first mission, on his first day in the unit. It devastated him.

The XO chuckled all day. The supply and personnel tent was still rolled up in the back of a truck.

How did the lieutenant feel when he found out the truth?

BRAVERY

Physical bravery is the baseline, not the grand achievement. Moral, ethical and professional bravery is less common and often more difficult. Leaders casually pledge their lives for an ideal, but refuse to endanger their career, evaluation report or friendship over such an issue.

"Bravery is a quality not to be dispensed with in the officers—like charity, it covers a great many defects."

—BENJAMIN STODDERT: LETTER TO JAMES SIMMONS, 13 DECEMBER 1798

MOTIVATION

A successful organization is not built on a few home run hitters who walk away from the plate a hero or a zero. Its foundation is the mass of people who can routinely hit a stand-up double.

"Do the common thing uncommonly well."

—PAUL OREFFICE, CHAIRMAN OF THE BOARD OF DOW CHEMICAL

INSPECTIONS

Traditionally, inspections ignore the many things done well, and endlessly publicize the few things done poorly. That's the easy approach, no insight or judgment required. Ignoring performance beyond the minimum required, while brutally punishing failure to meet that low standard, teaches your soldiers that meeting the minimum is the ONLY standard you care about.

A better technique may be to publicly praise outstanding accomplishment, and privately single out failures of effort. Even the worst units have several commendable accomplishments for every miserable failure.

"The art of being wise is the art of knowing what to overlook."

—WILLIAM JAMES

VIRTUES FOR LEADERS

The foundation of success can be found in the four leader virtues: Anticipation, Basic Leadership, Common Sense, Discipline.

Anticipation is what leaders are paid for. Properly executed, you will never have to "go to the sounds of the guns." *You will already be there.*

Your rank allows you to see a little farther than your subordinates, to *anticipate* missions, requirements and needs that are not yet apparent. Anticipation failure leads to "jump-through-your-ass-missions."

"The commander stands for the virtues of wisdom, sincerity, benevolence, courage and strictness."

—SUN ZSU

BASIC LEADERSHIP

Basic leadership. Be at the critical time and place. Lead by example. Enforce standards. Three simple steps, so seldom seen.

The brand new NCO knows what basic leadership is. He is on the perimeter with his soldiers, *before stand-to.* He personally checks his squad's LP/OP position. He personally inspects weapons. He checks the timing of the M2 machine gun because he knows it is important, and he knows how to do it (his commander does not know how to check and does not check). He *finds* the fault on the critical piece of equipment that the operator ignored on his PMCS because: "No one will check anyway."

Common sense is not so common after all. If something sounds stupid and looks stupid, perhaps it is.

Real Life

Chemical and conventional artillery fire destroyed the battalion TOC. The company commander in the alternate TOC became the unexpected commander of the brigade support area (BSA). His fear of making a mistake destroyed his common sense.

All M256 chemical detector kits reported negative results. The captain ordered unmasking procedures. His chemical NCO pointed out that the handful of remaining of BLUEFOR (friendly) tanks were dying quickly and the opposing force (OPFOR) armor would be in the BSA in a matter of minutes. He recommended immediate unmasking and evacuation, without unmasking procedures. The captain refused, noting that the standard operating procedure (SOP) did not allow it.

The captain was technically correct. That, however, would have been little comfort on a rainy afternoon at Arlington National Cemetery while the bugler played taps again and again.

Discipline is tempered with common sense.

Discipline is an uncommon virtue. The ability to impose and enforce standards on others is a product of their discipline. The will and the strength to impose and enforce standards on yourself is *self-discipline*. Self-discipline is the rarest of all the virtues; it is most often seen in those uncommon leaders who understand that everything in life is a graded event.

VISION

A clear vision, deep commitment and the ability to create the same in others mark an inspirational leader.

"Vision: the art of seeing things invisible."
—JONATHAN SWIFT

PEOPLE SELECTION

It is not hard to identify the top and bottom 10% of your subordinates; if you watch carefully, they will help you do it. It is the people in the middle who are tough to sort; and there is a big difference between soldiers in the 20th and the 80th percentile.

"You can observe a lot by just watching."
—YOGI BERRA

Some people perform best with only a goal and a timeline. Others need constant supervision. Your success depends on cultivating the former and recognizing the latter.

THE TYRANNY OF PERCEPTION

What your soldiers see of you they believe of you. Too often you believe only what you hear or read about them. You are both 50% wrong. You both believe you are 100% right.

Perception is reality, and it works in both directions. Successful anticipation of the critical time and place allows leaders to see the truth first hand.

LEADER PERSONALITIES

Everything in life is a graded event.

Soldiers watch, listen, and evaluate your every action.

Real Life

The outgoing battalion commander was the consummate "people person." He knew most of his soldiers' names as well as an amazing number of family members' names. His leaving was felt as a personal loss by the unit.

His success with motivational leadership left a big pair of shoes for the next guy to fill.

His replacement was very different. He was not interested in filling anybody's shoes. He was very effective at communicating his personal values and expectations. An indicator of how his soldiers perceived his values was reflected in the nickname he soon earned: The "Prince of Darkness."

The Army makes you a commander. Your soldiers make you a leader.

The evaluation the new commander received from the soldiers does not mean he was an ineffective commander in accomplishing the mission to a minimal standard. It may, however, be a reflection on his ability to *lead,* to inspire efforts beyond the norm.

The Army makes you a commander. Your soldiers make you a leader. What evaluation have you earned?

UNIT PERSONALITIES

Units have personalities too, often a reflection of the leadership.

Remember that leadership does not always mean the senior ranking individuals. Often the unit's self-chosen leader holds the real power.

Real Life

The radio told the young lieutenant that his platoon had only minutes to reach the helicopter or his men would walk home. He turned to his weary and heavily laden troops and signaled double time. Without exception, the tired soldiers turned toward the rear of the column and the platoon sergeant with the unspoken question of, "Do we?"

The lieutenant was the platoon leader, but he was not the platoon's leader. He had already lost the battle for real leadership.

PERCEPTION

Recognize that what seems perfectly obvious to you may be invisible from your soldiers' perspective.

Real Life

The lieutenant noticed two privates and a corporal who ignored trash as it blew past them. The young officer wanted to emphasize the obligation of the senior soldier in the group to take charge and enforce standards. He stopped and scolded them for not taking the initiative to pick up the trash and demanded to know, "Who is senior here?" As he prepared to dress down the bewildered corporal, one of the confused soldiers timidly replied, "Why you are, sir."

Consider your subordinate's perception.

KNOW YOUR UNIT

"Know Your Men—Know your Business—Know Yourself."

—MAJOR C.A. BACH 1917

You think you know everything about your unit; you are wrong. In the best units, involved leaders know a high percentage, but not all. In the worst units leaders are deaf, dumb, and blind. Dangerously dumb.

Real Life

Uninformed is unimportant.

He had brought his soldiers 1,000 miles to fight the Opposing Forces at the National Training Center. He thought he knew his soldiers. He thought he knew his unit. He was unaware of the cat that had deployed with them from Fort Lewis. He did know about the washing machine, banded to a pallet, dis-

charging precious drinking water onto the desert dust for the benefit of a select few.

He should have spent more time on patrol *inside* his unit.

LEADER SELECTION
Being in charge doesn't make you a leader. You don't select your unit's leaders. Your soldiers do. You can only strive to be the selectee.

"If you choose godly, honest men to be captains of horse, honest men will follow them."

—OLIVER CROMWELL: TO SIR WILLIAM SPRINGE, SEPTEMBER 1643

GREAT LEADERS
The great leader fosters an atmosphere of great expectations, heroic effort and personal commitment.

"The superior man is easy to serve and difficult to please."

—CONFUCIUS, ANALECTS, CIRCA 500 B. C.

INDICATORS OF EFFECTIVE LEADERSHIP
- Routine things happen routinely.
- Requests are obeyed as if they were orders, which in fact, they are.
- The leader is approachable and a good listener.
- He listens more than talks.
- When he does talk, people stop, look and listen, because they trust him and his judgment.
- He is not afraid to get dirty.
- He brags about his people, not himself.

"No man will make a great leader who wants to do it all himself, or to get all the credit for doing it."

—ANDREW CARNEGIE

- He is quick to accept the blame for failure but insists the credit for success belongs to his soldiers.
- He knows names (lots of them), including family members.
- Has strong convictions and makes them known.
- He trusts his people. They trust him.
- He always keeps his word (and therefore is careful about giving it).
- He is comfortable with people, and it shows.
- He is aware of everything, but not in charge of everything.
- He asks for recommendations when possible, and is not afraid of using them.

THE LEADERSHIP PARADOX

The paradox of leadership: The more you care about your mission and your soldiers, the better leader you are. However, when leadership is not measured by your boss (often only mission results are measured), any effort toward caring for soldiers uses time and energy that could be used to further your career.

In other words, in bad units with weak shortsighted raters and senior raters, being a committed leader puts you at a career disadvantage.

THE LEADER'S DILEMMA

Concern for soldiers and mission is the foundation of leadership. Too much of one or the other destroys leadership.

Soldiers will accept, even seek sacrifices if they feel it is justified and necessary. This implies communication, commitment and trust, in both directions.

> *Commitment to soldiers and dedication to the mission is the foundation of leadership.*

LEADERSHIP AND THE LAW OF NATURAL SELECTION

Every group has a leader. It is unavoidable. Even a ragged band of wanderers has a leader. It's the person who picks a direction and commands, "That way!"

> *"The question 'Who ought to be boss [leader]?' is like 'Who ought to be the tenor in the quartet?' Obviously, the man who can sing tenor."*
>
> —HENRY FORD

OBLIGATION OF PERSONAL RECOMMENDATION

You receive a tremendous vote of confidence when soldiers from other units come to you for advice and assistance. They do this because of your soldiers' personal recommendations.

Your soldiers are putting their reputation at risk with their peers because they feel you have value. Don't blow it.

QUITTING

"Defeat doesn't finish a man—quit does. A man is not finished when he's defeated. He's finished when he quits."

—RICHARD M. NIXON

Quitting is contagious. It reflects on the soldier and the weak leader who allowed him to quit.

You can order a soldier on a desperate assignment. You can watch him fail valiantly. You can join him on the hopeless mission. But you cannot allow him or yourself, to quit.

Real Life

Leaders don't allow themselves to quit.

It was late September, and the battalion was in a defensive field position on a remote Fort Hood training area. The Alpha Company commander approached the battalion commander and stated flatly, "Sir, I'm resigning and requesting release from active duty. I'd like to turn my company over to my XO, and get started on a resume."

The battalion commander absorbed this new development for a moment. He considered the impact on the 120 soldiers in Alpha Company. He thought of his obligation to their families, and his oath to the nation. Then he casually replied, "Sure, John."

Two substandard officers helping each other reach the lowest levels of professionalism.

NOT QUITTING

Actions certainly do speak louder than words.

> "Example is not the main thing in influencing others. It is the only thing."
>
> —ALBERT SCHWEITZER

Real Life

It was late Friday night. The platoon had been breaking tank track and replacing track shoes for hours. The soldiers were beyond exhaustion. They were beyond intimidation. They quit working and sat down, waiting for the inevitable ass-chewing.

The platoon sergeant had worked just as hard and long as they had. He was every bit as tired, and many years older. He approached the sullen group and said . . . nothing.

He walked past them as if they were invisible. He slowly bent down, picked up the tools and began to break track alone.

For several minutes the soldiers watched him sweat and grunt. Slowly, one by one, they each stood up and resumed work. Not a word was said, not then, not ever.

No amount of yelling or threats would have had the same effect. Soldiers' respect for him and his example drove them to push on.

The authority of his stripes would never have been as effective as the power of his *example*.

BENEFITS OF PERSONAL EXPERIENCE

Sometimes, only personal experience can teach a leadership lesson.

Real Life

The platoon sergeants assigned guards for their sector of the perimeter during the REFORGER winter training exercise. The first sergeant asked them how long each guard shift was. They replied, four hours. The senior NCO thought of the hip-deep snow and howling wind, then ordered each platoon sergeant to pull the first shift.

After an hour crouching in wet snow, the platoon sergeants were approaching hypothermia. The first sergeant called them in and asked again how long a shift should be. This answer was different.

LEADER DEVELOPMENT

"The graveyards are full of indispensable men."
—CHARLES DEGAULLE

What is the plan to improve the reading or writing skill of leaders who otherwise have good potential? If you are not sure this is a problem, take a look at your unit's written counseling records. They are a good indication of writing skills.

If a soldier truly wants to go to school, support him or her. The soldier will gladly do more than his or her fair share of work to have a schedule that accommodates at least some classes.

Are there any NCOs in your unit without an evaluation report in a leadership position? Why? If he or she has leadership potential, insist on a leadership position for the deserving soldier.

COMMANDER VS. LEADER

You are a commander because the Army saw value in you; you are not a leader until your soldiers feel the same. Value does not necessarily mean *like*. It does mean professional respect and trust.

"No man is a leader until his appointment is ratified in the minds and hearts of his men."

—THE INFANTRY JOURNAL, AUGUST 1948

A commander forces compliance.

A leader inspires commitment.

Compliance can be coerced.

Commitment must be earned.

PLANNING

Make it simple. Keep it simple. To paraphrase George Patton: A good plan executed violently today is better than a great plan next week. Resist the temptation to add bells and whistles until the whole thing falls apart.

"Long-range planning does not deal with future decisions, but with the future of present decisions."

—PETER DRUCKER

There are two types of people in this world: those who make long-range plans, and those who work for those who make long-range plans. Which one are you?

POWER

No pain = no power.

Know the difference between power and authority. Authority is a legal right. Power is the ability to get things done.

When the chips are down, which person do you go to for help—the one with power or authority?

By the way, if the person with power also has authority, he or she is a mighty person indeed.

POWER DOWN

"Expect people to be better than they are; it helps them to become better. But don't be disappointed when they are not; it helps them to keep trying."

—MARY BROWNE, NATIONAL ENQUIRER

"POWER DOWN" is a buzzword that many preach but few practice.

Do not tell subordinate leaders how to do it. Assign the objective and make your junior leaders take charge. Beware, this incurs risk. You must judge how much guidance will allow a soldier to successfully complete the mission while allowing maximum room to grow. You will sometimes be disappointed, and often be tempted to direct his actions in greater detail. You must accept the risk of failure, so that he may learn from his mistakes.

THE POWER OF PRAISE

"Sandwich every bit of criticism between two layers of praise."

—MARY KAY ASH, MARY KAY ON PEOPLE MANAGEMENT

Effective praise is not the empty gesture of undeserved award. It is the recognition of superior effort or results by a respected leader. Your people don't work harder or longer for a mere paycheck. They work harder than they have to, because they want to, because of you.

Whom you choose to recognize, and why, is carefully scrutinized by your people. They know who is the hardest working, or most effective, or most proficient person in your organization. This is a test to see if you know.

COMMAND PRESENCE

Presence is more than just being there; walk slowly, speak calmly, appear confident. This inspires the same in your soldiers.

When emotions run high, the leader is calm. When hope is gone, he is optimistic, powerful and commanding.

"One of the most valuable qualities of a commander is a flair for putting himself in the right place at the vital time."

—FIELD MARSHAL
SIR WILLIAM SLIM,
UNOFFICIAL HISTORY, 1959

PRIORITIES

Personal time is the leader's most precious resource. Where he spends his time is an indicator of what is actually important to him.

"Make service your first priority, not success and success will follow."

—AUTHOR UNKNOWN

Real Life

The new brigade commander briefed every company commander in his unit. He said, "If you never see me again you are doing a good job. You'll get an Army Commendation Medal and a one-block evaluation report when you leave command. If I call you to my office, you are in very serious trouble. If I show up in your unit area, you can tear off your captains bar, because you are through."

This colonel meant exactly what he said. He felt that meetings and e-mail provided sufficient "command presence" to ensure compliance. He was right. He earned a superior evaluation report and a promotion, for his performance as a peacetime commander.

Remember though, that mere compliance may not be enough in combat. Men and women don't die for compliance, only for commitment.

PERSONAL PRIORITIES

Even the most dedicated soldier must balance the continuous demands of selfless service and the requirements of a successful personal life. If you are foolish enough to disregard your own personal life, you must guard against disregarding the personal lives of your subordinates.

"The young soldier boasted: 'I have two wives, the Army, and my second wife.' The old soldier replied, 'One of your wives will surely leave you in time, you should endeavor that both don't.'"

—A ROTATIONAL SOLDIER AND OC AT NTC, AUTUMN 1996

Real Life

The new battalion commander was the first officer to leave every evening. He noticed that the parking lot was always full when he departed. He recognized this as the legacy of his predecessor.

The colonel held a meeting with his staff officers, and explained, "If you must work until 2200 every night to finish your work, then I am asking too much of you, and you should tell me. If you are just too in-

efficient to finish your work at a reasonable time, rest assured, I will tell you." He paused, then added, *"There are no bonus points for working one hundred hours a week, gentlemen."*

No one believed him. They had witnessed the unpleasant repercussions of the previous commander when people left before sundown.

Once they accepted that he meant what he said, they redoubled their efforts during the day, and found new efficiencies. They did this because they were now graded on results, not time.

PRIVILEGE AND THE PRICE OF LEADERSHIP

Rank has its privileges. For real leaders it also has sacrifices and responsibilities.

"It is not titles that honor men but men that honor titles."

—MACHIAVELLI

Real Life

It had been a successful rotation at the National Training Center, but the toughest battle, equipment turn-in, was behind schedule. In an effort to focus his soldier's efforts, the brigade commander placed the main post off limits to the entire brigade.

The Support Battalion commander had planned a victory dinner with key leaders at the Officers Club.

He sought and received special dispensation from the brigade commander for his key officers and NCOs to dine on main post, although his soldiers could not. Only one leader declined to attend.

The battalion commander summoned that lone captain and expressed his grave displeasure over a "non-team player."

What did the young captain gain? His rater was angry. He embarrassed his peers. His soldiers would never know what he had done.

What would you do?

PROMISES

"Never promise anything you can't deliver."

—ANONYMOUS

Do not say it if you do not mean it. Move heaven and earth to keep it.

Make promises with caution; keep them always. This is tracked in the hearts and minds of your soldiers, peers and seniors. You can only blow it once.

REENLISTMENT

"The time to start reenlisting a good man is when he first joins your unit."

—GENERAL BRUCE C. CLARKE

Remember the way your present unit welcomed you? Would it make you want to reenlist to remain in it? If so, are you ensuring that all new soldiers receive the same great reception? If not, what have you done to correct it?

Real Life

Phantom Warriors, Indeed
The brigade was dead last in reenlistment rates. A key factor was the cooks. Virtually no cooks in the forward units reenlisted. They hated the continual deployments and field duty. Obvious exceptions were the cooks assigned to the Main Support Battalion. Their reduced field commitments were reflected in their substantial reenlistment rate.

Cooks in the forward units refused to reenlist unless they were transferred to the Main Support Battalion. The brigade sergeant major agreed.

When the number of cooks in the Main Support Battalion exceeded the authorized strength, the Sergeant Major assigned them to the forward units, with duty at the Main Support Battalion. This left the Main Support Battalion with more cooks than needed or authorized and a reduced work schedule. The forward units had fewer cooks and increased work schedules, further aggravating the reenlistment problem in the forward units.

The sergeant major screwed soldiers in the forward units to make the brigade's reenlistment rates look better. Do you think that is the first or last time he traded integrity for numbers?

THE EASY WAY IS ALWAYS WRONG

"Following the path of least resistance is what makes rivers and men crooked."

—ANONYMOUS

The easy way is always wrong. It is easier to sleep in than attend physical training (PT), easier to drink coffee in the tactical operations center (TOC) van than to walk the perimeter during early morning stand-to, easier to ignore an ethics or leadership failure than to act on it. The easy way is always wrong.

TRUST, BUT VERIFY

"Trust in Allah, but tie your camel."

—OLD MUSLIM PROVERB

You must trust your subordinates. Do not, however, doubt your responsibility to check. It is a leader's responsibility to check everything. Your subordinate leaders must understand that.

Check to provide recognition for things done well. This demonstrates your intent to find the good things as well as areas to improve. Under normal conditions you should provide two pats on the back for every kick in the butt. When soldiers believe they can not meet your standards, they quit trying.

Real Life

Trust, but Verify
The sergeant had performed flawlessly as battalion operations NCO. The operations officer (S3) pur-

chased a plaque to present to him at his farewell luncheon. The farewell included many heartfelt accolades, followed by an emotional parting.

Several weeks later the property book officer (PBO) called the S3 regarding a computer the S3 had personally signed for. The S3 said that his recently departed NCO had returned the computer a month before. The PBO paused, then replied, "There is no record of it being returned."

A SOLDIER'S TRUST
Soldiers must trust their leaders. They must believe leaders will not squander their lives, or even their sweat.

This trust is common in the dedication and enthusiasm of new soldiers. Poor leaders in a young soldier's first unit will quickly lose their trust.

Subordinates build their trust on their assessment of you. Their evaluations will be what you do and fail to do, what you say and fail to say, what you tolerate and what you refuse to tolerate, what you reward and what you punish. The picture that emerges from these actions is a window on your character.

"The foundation of leadership is character." [A strong character builds trust.]
—GENERAL ALEXANDER M. PATCH

EFFECTIVE
LEADERSHIP

SUBORDINATE TRUST

THEIR EXPERIENCE
WITH YOU

THEIR CONFIDENCE
IN YOU

THEIR CONTACT TIME
WITH YOU

THEIR PRIOR DECISIONS
AND ACTIONS

Real Life

A group of soldiers trained in a large field on Fort
Benning, Georgia. It was the end of a blazing hot
day. The sweat-soaked men were exhausted. They
were sitting in the wood-line seeking shelter from the
sun when the lieutenant approached.

The officer said, "I need a volunteer to walk to
the range shack with two five-gallon water jugs, and
bring them back full. There is no vehicle available,
but I need the water now." The weary soldiers looked
at the shack several hundred yards away and at the
ankle-deep sand to be traversed with the full jugs. No
one answered.

Finally, one soldier stood and said, "I'll do it, sir." For several seconds the officer said nothing, then he asked, "Why would you volunteer for such a miserable task?"

The young man replied, "If an officer is asking, then it must be very important."

Do your soldiers still have that level of faith in you?

THINKING

Think, then do, always in that sequence.

An extra two minutes checking your protractor work saves thirty minutes lost on the compass course.

> *"Think like a man of action; act like a man of thought."*
> —HENRI LOUIS BERGSON

TAKING CHARGE

It is easy taking charge of the exceptional unit or the truly horrible unit. It is the mediocre unit that's most difficult.

The exceptional unit has a recent history of achieving great things. They may have identified with those achievements and the previous leader. The previous leader may have earned the devotion of soldiers and leaders. The astute newcomer assumes responsibility quietly, professionally, and makes changes with caution. Your changes must not be viewed as a rebuke of past practices, only an improvement that builds upon them.

> *"Uncertainty will always be part of the taking-charge process."*
> —HAROLD GENEEN

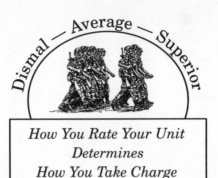

Dismal — Average — Superior

How You Rate Your Unit
Determines
How You Take Charge

The dismal unit has no successes to cling to. They have no proud history with the last leader. They have no confidence in themselves. They want to believe in someone. You must convince them it is you. Assume command and control with determination and strength. Impose your will and demand response. Begin with subordinate leaders. Immediately establish and enforce strict standards. Any ethical or legal standards that differentiate you from your predecessor will do; then find someone to publicly reward for doing it. The intent is to impose your will, and establish your presence. Improvement must come quickly, to retain your credibility.

The mediocre unit is the most difficult to undertake. The soldiers have no perception of being a "bad" unit. Indeed, they may hold your predecessor in high regard for not enforcing stricter standards. Being average may be good enough for them. You must build on the good that is already there. Evaluate your leaders, soldiers, and mission. Reward the good, train those with potential, and eliminate the bad. Improvement will come, but only with time.

TAKING CHARGE TIMELINE

When does taking charge begin? The first time soldiers see you. From that day on, your every action will be recorded, discussed and evaluated. Not simply because you are a potential leader, but because all people continually evaluate those around them.

If your tenure as a battalion staff officer was less than impressive, don't think you are starting with a clean slate when you take command of a company. Your successes and failures will precede you. If you don't believe it, remember when you were told of a new supervisor, or leader coming to your unit. The first thing you asked was, "What do you know about him?"

Everything in life is a graded event.

TEAM BUILDING

You cannot be a star without recognition. The most powerful recognition does not consist in medals and certificates. It dwells in the respect of people you admire. It is the acknowledgment that each individual has a special role to fill and does so to a very high standard.

"The real trick in building a team is to have 25 individual stars on it."
—TOM PETERS

"The strength of the pack is the wolf, and the strength of the wolf is the pack."

—RUDYARD KIPLING

This is far more than your squad, platoon, or company. When appropriate, the wise leader includes his or her family support group, public affairs representative, property book team and other outside groups that provide support for the unit in all company activities. This invitation is seldom offered and always appreciated.

DEVELOPING SUBORDINATES

"The only way to develop responsibility in people is to give them responsibility."

—KENNETH BLANCHARD

Select outstanding people. Give them a mission Give them an azimuth and get out of the way. Stand by with guidance and recognition at critical points. Ensure they understand your intent. Reward success; build on failure.

You won't have a full set of top performers. You must develop them. Encourage everyone in your organization to set challenging goals and meet them. Define and quantify these goals by periodic counseling. Publicly recognize achievements based on the difficulty of the mission and the rank, training and experience of the soldier. Your personal interest may make the difference between mediocre and outstanding.

THE NEW GUY

"When duty whispers low, thou must, the youth replies, I can."

—R. W. EMERSON: VOLUNTARIES, 1867

First impressions are lasting.

Who is responsible for the care of new soldiers? You are! While NCOs do indeed make it happen, it is the senior person's responsibility. Go to the barracks and see new soldiers on their first night. Let them know that you know they are there and that they are part of a good unit.

Use a standardized in-processing welcome letter. Areas include: appearance, PT, weight control, inspections, POV safety and policy, punctuality, chain of command, and safety. Brief all new personnel. Use slides and handouts to describe the unit and its mission.

Invite spouses and bring some of your unit's spouses in to meet them. This does not replace the initial personal interview on arrival.

THE SECRET OF EXPECTATIONS

Most people do what you expect them to do. If you expect mediocre performance they will not disappoint you. If you demand high standards and hard work, most people will rise to the challenge.

"High expectations are the key to everything."
—SAM WALTON

The second group may fail, but not due to lack of interest, concern, or effort. You must tend these growing young leaders as a master gardener would. Provide nourishment when required. Give critical evaluation when needed. Weed your garden if you must.

THE POWER OF EXAMPLE

"Words that do not match deeds are not important."

—ERNESTO CHE GUEVARA

You must give 100% of yourself if you expect the same from your soldiers. This includes squeezing out that last two push-ups during physical training, walking through the motor pool one more time before going home after a long day, stopping by the barracks or hospital on the way home, being the first into the frigid swimming pool for drown-proofing, eating last, and a hundred other things that you do not want to do, but know you should.

Real Life

Warm words and holiday spirit filled the mess hall during the battalion Thanksgiving meal. The officers and senior NCOs were magnificent in their dress blue uniforms. The young soldiers and their families took advantage of an inexpensive feast during the financially difficult holiday period.

The unit cohesiveness and mutual trust found in that shared meal was real, until the leadership dropped the ball on the one-yard line.

As soldiers and their families began to drift toward the door, several young officers gathered at the cornucopia display. Some filled their pockets with fruit and nuts. Those with less dignity took cloth napkins from the tables to wrap up greater quantities of stolen goods.

This sad performance played to a semicircle of be-wildered children whose enlisted parents had admon-ished them not to touch the display. These were parents who could not provide the same treat at home on their smaller salaries.

REPUTATION AND LEADERSHIP

Leaders can be hated, or feared, and still be effective. The one thing they cannot with-stand is ridicule.

Real Life

The platoon had marched a dozen miles in the Geor-gia sun and still had a dozen to go. Each soldier car-ried a medium rucksack stuffed with equipment weighing half his body weight. The platoon leader was a small man, who carried a large rucksack that was obviously bursting at the seams.

As the weary men protested, their leader berated them for carrying less than him and complaining more. They silently accepted his tirade, shamed by the huge rucksack that only he carried.

At a water stop the men grounded their ruck-sacks. When the platoon leader walked away, a disgruntled soldier kicked his large rucksack. He stared in disbelief as it slid several feet. He opened it to find only a sleeping bag, weighing less than ten pounds.

The platoon leader returned to find his secret revealed and his reputation destroyed. A new and popular nickname for the former leader quickly spread: Nerf Ruck.

THE FIVE PERCENT SOLUTION

Any good first sergeant can handle 95% of the company commander's responsibility. The commander gets paid for the final five percent.

He is paid for answers when there don't seem to be any right answers, for decisions when there is not enough information to decide, and for action, when any action seems to be wrong. He must look beyond the facts and figures, the charts and projections. He must see the humanity in the worst of us and the potential in the least of us. He must balance what is legal against what is just, what is best for the many against what is right for the few.

He must be firm when all others waiver. He must demonstrate courage and character when it is clearly not in his own best interest. He must be more than he appears to be, and he must appear to be everything that is needed.

SLEEP PLAN

Sleep is the "eleventh class of supply." Effective management requires a plan. It must be more than a paper drill that leaders neither participate in nor enforce. Leaders at all levels must ensure subordinates do not remain awake as long a possible in order to make a few more fatigue-clouded decisions before succumbing to exhaustion.

"No human being knows how sweet sleep is but a soldier."
—COLONEL JOHN S. MOSBY

SOCIALIZING WITH SUBORDINATES

It is true that familiarity breeds contempt. No one wants to be ordered into a high-risk mission by "Doug," but may be honored by such an order from General Douglas MacArthur.

Familiarity is a one-way street; once traveled, you can not turn back. Do not confuse familiarity with personal leadership. The former is a destructive relationship; the latter a vital part of superior organizations.

"I command—or I hold my tongue."
—NAPOLEON

NEW SERGEANTS OR CORPORALS

This is the toughest promotion. Your new NCO was a junior enlisted soldier yesterday. Today he must enforce unpopular standards on his former peers.

The NCOs may not immediately accept him or her. If he or she is doing his job he or she has already alienated his old friends. He or she is left with no support from either

"We have good corporals and sergeants, and some good lieutenants and captains, and those are far more important than good generals."
—GENERAL WILLIAM TECUMSEH SHERMAN

group. Only the strongest NCO can survive in that situation. The average human will lapse into old, familiar relationships with former peers; you will have lost a NCO and gained a mere sergeant.

You must ensure that new leaders are treated differently, just as they treat their soldiers differently.

Never include an E5 with E1-E4 for privileges, personal equipment inventory (TA-50), or other tasks. Segregate your new NCO as soon as possible in the barracks, preferably to another building, or at least another floor.

Sergeant: The toughest promotion.

Real Life

Every NCO in the battalion stood at attention and watched, as the command sergeant major presented the new NCO with his framed, signed copy of the NCO creed. After the applause died away, he handed the young man a roster of every NCO in the battalion, with their work and home phone numbers, and said, "These are your brothers and sisters; call on them any time day or night." He turned to the formation and declared, "This man is your concern. His success is your success. Each of us has a personal responsibility for him; now get up here and tell him!" The crowd erupted in clapping and yelling as they surged forward to engulf the young man.

RIGHTS CARD

Real Life

The staff duty officer checked the field-training site. The guards smelled of alcohol. He found two cans of beer in the shadows near their tent; still cold. He asked if it was theirs. They replied, "Yes." He relieved them of duty.

The officer failed to read them their rights before asking if the beer belonged to them. The miscreant soldiers escaped punishment on this technicality. The officer did not escape the wrath of his commander for his bungling.

DOING THE RIGHT THING

Some people always do right; some always do wrong. You cannot change either group. The 80% in the middle are your challenge. When you make it harder for them to do the right thing than the wrong thing, they will not do the right thing.

> "Character is doing the right thing when nobody's looking. There are too many people who think that the only thing that's right is to get by, and the only thing that's wrong is to get caught."
>
> —J. C. WATTS

Tales of your successes will grow over beer in the barracks. So will your failures.

YOUR REPUTATION

Your reputation is built 10% on how you achieve success and 90% on how you deal with adversity and failure. Your passion is your passport to leadership.

Your reputation is built both on your achievements and the achievements of others. As you are recognized and rewarded, you must do the same for your team.

Reputations and legends are built on the margins of your behavior, not the workaday stuff. Nobody cares how many memos you typed today. They do care that you hold officers to the same standards as enlisted soldiers, and that you hold yourself to the highest standard of all.

PERSONAL RESPONSIBILITY

Where does your personal responsibility for soldiers end?

Real Life

An artillery attack at the National Training Center left many wounded soldiers on the ground waiting for first aid. A young officer stood among the injured soldiers doing nothing. When a sergeant asked why he wasn't helping, the man replied, "These are not my soldiers."

The Answer: Your personal responsibility for soldiers never ends.

MOTIVATION

Recognition is the magic ingredient for motivation—not necessarily awards or even public praise, but appreciation and recognition from people they *value*.

"At the bottom of things, most people want to be understood and appreciated."

—FROM THE TEACHINGS OF BUDDHA

REALITY

Real Life

The soldiers had "died" in a mock battle at the National Training Center. They now relaxed and laughed at the mortuary affairs tent. The next 24 hours they could talk, eat, and sleep.

The company commander entered the tent. He found his soldier and listened as the young man laughed about his untimely "death" due to his poorly maintaining equipment.

The captain approached the smiling soldier and began to speak. His words painted a vivid picture for the young private: a sunny Sunday morning, his mother answering the door to find a chaplain in uniform, the unimaginable pain she felt, the lifetime of anguish she faced, the tears on his grave at Christmas and Easter.

No one in the tent was laughing now. The young soldier was sobbing . . . as he should have been.

"The ultimate security is your understanding of reality."

—H. STANLEY JUDD

NAMES

"If you remember my name . . . you indicate that I have made an impression on you. Remember my name and you add to my feeling of importance."

—DALE CARNEGIE

The most beautiful sound to anyone is his or her own name. Think of the best leader you have ever known. How many names did he or she know?

Names are golden coins, to be spent only at the appropriate time. Learn everybody's. Keep notes if you must.

BAD LEADERS

"I don't have time to distinguish between the unfortunate and the incompetent.

—GENERAL CURTIS LEMAY

There are many bad leaders—the politician, the careerist, and many others. Some are inept, amoral, or just plain stupid. They are all dangerous.

The captain and lieutenant who buried live ammunition on Fort Benning's Red Cloud Range are just one example. Although the culpable lieutenant suffered so much regret that he confessed, ruining his career and his boss's, he still committed the crime. When faced with doing the right thing or the obviously wrong thing that his boss told him to do, he chose the easy wrong.

His confession may mitigate his punishment, but he can never regain his professional integrity. His credibility as a leader was ruined.

TOLERANCE OF MISTAKES

Mistakes are the product of action and judgment. If you don't allow subordinates to take independent action, their limited judgment poses no threat to you. However, you subordinates won't be much help to you either.

You want subordinates to take thoughtful, decisive action when necessary. Even if they are sometimes wrong.

"You must be able to underwrite the honest mistakes of your subordinates if you wish to develop their initiative and experience."

—GENERAL BRUCE C. CLARKE

Real Life

The assistant operations officer made a huge mistake. It reflected badly on the unit, particularly the operations officer himself. Soon a very angry brigade commander arrived. The young assistant tried to take responsibility, but was brushed aside by the senior officer, who ordered everyone to stand at attention as he delivered fifteen minutes of humiliating public abuse to the operations officer. The brigade commander left, and the operations officer called his misguided assistant into his office.

The younger man stood at quivering attention. His boss said quietly, "Have a seat." then, "Have you learned anything from this?" The senior officer listened to a tremulous explanation, nodded, and replied, "Good job. Get back to work."

LEADER VS. MANAGER

"A leader knows what's best to do; a manager merely knows how best to do it."

—KEN ADELMAN

Leader and manager, you've got to be both to be successful. A leader who cannot manage his assets quickly has not assets. A manager who cannot lead may be efficient, but he will not be effective.

Both traits are necessary, but neither is effective in all situations. You must know when, and how much of each, to apply. In times of crisis, or unknown threats and opportunities, leader traits are needed to provide guidance and vision, as well at take risks to leverage opportunity.

Managership tries to eliminate unknowns and risks. It attempts to become very efficient in routine tasks. The specter of risk may blind managers to opportunity.

Both traits are needed.

LEADER VS. MANAGER TRAITS

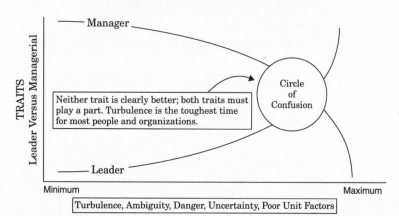

Manager

TRAITS
Leader Versus Managerial

Circle of Confusion

Neither trait is clearly better; both traits must play a part. Turbulence is the toughest time for most people and organizations.

Leader

Minimum   Maximum

Turbulence, Ambiguity, Danger, Uncertainty, Poor Unit Factors

SNIVEL GEAR

If officers personally purchase expensive civilian cold-weather gear, how do they know when their privates on duty in the rain are overexposed in their issue gear? They know that an E2 with three kids is not ordering high-speed stuff from the Cav Store.™ While they are blissfully unaware, he becomes a cold-weather injury. His family expects better stewardship; so does the United States Army.

Managers strive for efficiency in routine operations. Leaders seek effectiveness in times of crisis.

—PARAPHRASED FROM
MAJOR CHARLES ANDRE

LITTLE WHITE LIES

Lies are never little, never white, and never free.

"A single lie destroys a whole reputation for integrity."

—BALTASAR GRACI
·N Y MORALES, THE ART OF
WORLDLY WISDOM, 1647

ROOMMATE HATE

Roommate assignment is too often a casual decision that has tremendous impact on soldiers and units. Roommate selection should be as carefully considered as sponsorship. In the best units, it is.

Real Life

Privates First Class Smith and Jones hated each other. An initial dislike had grown under the pressurized requirements of sharing a barracks room. Now they stood on front of the commander for fighting.

Each claimed the other had started the brawl. One had paid the phone deposit; the other had paid the cable TV deposit. Neither wanted to lose his deposit, and insisted the other had to move out of the room. Each chain of command supported its soldier's version of the story. The first sergeant recommended both be moved.

The commander tried to find justice among the tangled accusations. He ordered both miscreants to adjourn to the hallway and decide if they both wanted to stay or they both wanted to move.

They both moved.

The malassigned roommates no longer had to live together, but they had to work together, creating additional problems. A more thoughtful choice of roommates would have avoided this mess.

SOLDIER OF THE MONTH

Soldier and NCO of the Month should have their pictures on the wall of your unit and your parent unit. Your public affairs representative should arrange a photo and article in the post newspaper. A letter to the soldier's spouse or parents from the unit leadership is a powerful reinforcement.

PROFESSIONAL COMPETENCE

THE CHAIN OF COMMAND

Don't be misled. There is only one *chain of command*. It runs from the president through each level of command. The command sergeant major, the first sergeant, and the platoon sergeant are not in the chain of command—but they are in the NCO *support channel*, which is parallel and complementary to the chain of command. Both are communication channels used to pass information up and down. Neither is a one-way street, nor are the two entirely separate. In order for the chain of command to work, the NCO support channel must also be operating.

DELEGATION

Authority is *supposed* to be delegated. You *want* subordinates to make it happen without your personal intervention. The more you delegate and coach, the better subordi-

"Strange as it sounds, great leaders gain authority by giving it away."

—VICE ADMIRAL JAMES STOCK-
DALE, *MILITARY ETHICS*, 1987

nates will use your authority. The better they use your authority, the less need for your coaching, and the more time you have available for other priorities.

COMPETITION MANAGEMENT

"The healthiest
competition occurs when
average people win by
putting in above-average
effort."

—COLON POWELL,

Power of positive competition is great. It pushes people to work harder and smarter, and provides a sense of camaraderie when the individual and the team win.

The danger of corrosive competition is also great, because it can destroy trust and poison relationships. It descends into winning by any means, and places reward for the winning individual over the good of the team.

The smart leader harnesses the power of competition and controls its destructive potential.

Real Life

The battalion commander told his lieutenants that his evaluation would place them into one of three categories. The first (and largest) group were those officers who had done a good to very good job. The next group was for the best performers in the battalion. His third and highest rating was reserved for those who had done the most to help their fellow lieutenants.

The effect of this commander's performance evaluation philosophy was dramatic. In contrast to other units, when one of his companies had an inspection, every lieutenant in the battalion would converge to ensure the company was ready.

THE ULTIMATE CORRECTION

Write a soldier's family, spouse, or parents to assure them of your interest in the success of their soldier. Asking their assistance in correcting behavior is effective only for the fence sitters.

Such a letter is a powerful tool for the right soldier but destructive when used for the wrong soldier. Use with caution.

TIMING

Real Life

The youthful soldier crossed the PX parking lot with his wife. An officer hurried behind him, intent on delivering a scalding admonishment for his jacket, which hung open against regulations. As the soldier approached the doors a senior noncommissioned officer noticed the open jacket and the angry officer. The furious officer caught the sergeant's eye and pointed to the jacket. The NCO nodded, followed the couple inside and . . . waited.

Never correct a soldier in front of his family.

The young couple separated inside the PX. The NCO approached the soldier, who quickly closed his jacket.

The angry officer stopped the NCO and demanded, "Why didn't you correct that man sooner!" The wise sergeant calmly replied, "Never correct a man in front of his family, sir."

THE EXECUTION OF UNPOPULAR ORDERS

Execute all decisions as if they were your own. Require the same of your subordinates.

This is easy to say, but hard to do. You will be powerless to enforce this if you slip, even once, in the way you present unpopular missions or requirements to your subordinates.

The less popular the requirement, the more critical your presentation.

PARTICIPATION OF SUBORDINATES

Simple routine things require almost no thought. Unusual or abnormal requirements need more creativity and participation by subordinates.

Listen to your subordinate leaders, when possible, before making far-reaching decisions. Let them persuade you to do it the way you wanted to anyway. They will all be committed to your goal because it is *their* goal.

WHEN TO MAKE DECISIONS

Decisiveness counts more than accuracy—up to a point.

There is a time for immediate, decisive action. There is also a time for reflective, thoughtful consultation with your people before acting. Your success lies in recognizing the difference.

At what point must you "decide to decide?" You will never have all the pertinent information you might want to consider. You have to determine how much information is enough for a good decision. Notice the word *good,* not perfect. To paraphrase General George Patton: "A good decision today is better than a perfect decision next week."

"Successful leaders have the courage to take action where others hesitate."

—AUTHOR UNKNOWN

THE IMPACT OF PERSONAL INTEREST

If something is important to your soldiers, it should be important to you. A leader asking about personal or professional issues in a soldier's life is powerful. The implied task is that you know something about a soldier's life, and demonstrate that you care.

Real Life

The sergeant was failing the physical fitness test. She has successfully completed the push-ups and sit-ups, but her pace on the two-mile run was far too slow.

As she reached the halfway point, her squad leader joined her. He ran in silence for a minute, then turned to the young single mother and said; "If Julia was here, she would ride her bike alongside you. She would call out to you, 'Come on, mommy, we can do it.' You would pick up your pace, because you can't let her down. Again she would say, 'Come on, mommy, we can do it.' And you would do it, because you can't let her see you fail."

She passed the test, only because the NCO knew the name of her daughter.

DELEGATION

> *"No man will make a great leader who wants to do it all himself, or to get all the credit for doing it."*
> —ANDREW CARNEGIE

This is your goal. You want to be able to delegate to competent, confident leaders and subordinates. How do you achieve this? Coaching and counseling builds confident, competent leaders.

You are a successful coach when your soldiers feel they have done it all themselves. That builds confidence. Counseling reinforces successes and outlines areas to improve. That builds competence.

COMMAND CLIMATE—
ZERO DEFECTS

Do not foster a "zero defect" atmosphere. No one can grow in that environment. Soldiers must have (limited) freedom to fail. Do not reprimand a soldier for making a bad decision if it was genuinely his or her best effort possible under the circumstances. Do, however, reprimand for not making a necessary decision when he or she was senior.

> *"You must be able to underwrite the honest mistakes of your subordinates if you wish to develop their initiative and experience."*
>
> —GENERAL BRUCE C. CLARKE

PLANNING

KISS (Keep it Simple, Stupid)

As a trainer at NTC once said, "A simple plan with few decision points allow leaders to concentrate on execution." Sound's good, doesn't it?

> *"Everything should be made as simple as possible, but not simpler."*
>
> —ALBERT EINSTEIN

SUPERVISION

Real Life

The commander had painted each of his buildings in Army camouflage. The battalion commander loved it. The director of public works did not. He ordered the buildings repainted in standard white. The commander and first sergeant directed that soldiers on extra duty repaint the buildings.

The staff duty NCO supervised the detail. His supervision was minimal. The detail's boredom was great. They began to paint "FTA" and "This sucks,"(among other things) on the buildings and

If you will not devote the time to properly supervise your soldiers, you cannot complain about the results.

paint over the words before quitting time. They began to enjoy the detail.

They became more artistic, and more graphic. They added some rather-impressive artwork. It was great fun. Then, with sixty feet of artistic statement in-place on a building facing a major road, they ran out of white paint.

It was September. There was no additional paint on hand. There would be no money to purchase until October. It was a long month.

ORDERS

"Issuing orders is worth about 10 percent. The remaining 90 percent consists in assuring proper and vigorous execution of the order."

—GENERAL
GEORGE S. PATTON. JR.

A "request" by a senior is the same as an order, and in the best units it is treated as such. Routine things happen routinely, without discussion.

In strong units a request is treated as an order . . . because it is. In weak units an order is treated as a request, because it is.

HABIT

"Nothing is stronger than habit."

—OVID, *"AMORES,"* CIRCA AD 5

Do it the right way every time.

Real Life

The field problem had been a misery of icy rain and mud. The battalion commander announced that he was canceling the rest of the exercise. Each comman-

der could immediately release half of his company to
return to main post; the remainder would depart the
next day.

As a young captain and his first sergeant left the
meeting, the NCO asked, "Which platoons will you
release tonight, sir?" The officer paused, then replied,
"We're all staying, Top. We came out as a unit and
that is the way we'll go back." The pair walked qui-
etly for a moment, then the first sergeant smiled and
softly said, "I think you are gonna be all right, sir."

ATTENTION TO DETAIL

Every soldier you meet is your responsibility. Check every soldier you see, regardless of whom he works for, for compliance with Army appearance standards. Ask a driver if he has done his vehicle maintenance checks (periodic maintenance, checks and services, or "PMCS"). He will always say, "Yes." Then take him outside and have him show you the oil level or water or anything else. You will reinforce standards and gain a reputation as a detail man.

FAVORITISM

If subordinates can tell that a leader personally likes them, or dislikes them, that leader has failed. His or her obligation is to be

"In the end, it is attention to detail that makes all the difference. It's the center fielder's extra two steps to the left, the salesman's memory for names, the lover's phone call, the soldier's clean weapon. It is the thing that separates the winners from the losers, the men from the boys and very often the living from the dead."

—DAVID NOONAN

"... an officer on duty
knows no one—to be
partial is to dishonor
both himself and the
object of his Ill-advised
favor."

—BREVET MAJOR WILLIAM JENKINS
WORTH, BATTALION ORDERS,
WEST POINT, NEW YORK,
22 DECEMBER 1820

strictly impartial and professional toward every soldier. Even the misimpression of favoritism damages leadership.

When a subordinate feels that a dangerous or unpopular mission has been assigned due to personal bias, it destroys the leader's credibility, and the subordinate's commitment.

EXPERTISE

Only an expert can know when to break the rules. Are you an expert?

"There is a great
difference between
knowing a thing and
understanding it."

—CHARLES KETTERING WITH
T. A. BOYD, PROPHET OF PROGRESS

GLOBAL POSITIONING SYSTEM

With a GPS the chance of being lost (embarrassed) is nearly zero. That is why many GPS's stay locked up in the vehicles of senior leaders while the privates and specialists who actually need them do not have them.

GPS is a great tool, but it's not the only tool. It can be a dangerous crutch that disappears with the loss of a 25-cent battery. You still need a map and compass, and the skill to use them.

FRIENDS

"Be courteous to all, but
intimate with few; and
let those few be well
tried before you give
them your confidence."

—GEORGE WASHINGTON

Your selection of friends is a direct reflection on your standards, values and ethics. This may not be fair, but it is true.

TIMELINESS

A good officer once said, "If you are always early, then you are never late." After your butt has been shredded and your hard-won reputation for dependability has been damaged, you will better understand this bit of ancient wisdom.

". . . go sir, gallop, and don't forget that the world was made in six days. You can ask me for anything you like, except time."

—NAPOLEON BONAPARTE

APOLOGY

An apology may be appropriate and appreciated, but the root cause is usually a failure of character. You cannot acknowledge that more than once.

"An officer should never apologize to his men; also an officer should never be guilty of an act for which his sense of justice tells him he should apologize."

—MAJOR C.A. BACH, "KNOW YOUR MEN—KNOW YOUR BUSINESS—KNOW YOURSELF." ADDRESS TO NEW OFFICERS, 1917

MORAL INDIFFERENCE

Moral indifference is not neutral. To know of wrongdoing and not act to prevent or punish it, is to condone it. To condone such behavior is to become part of it. To be part of shameful behavior destroys leadership credibility.

The first half of the well-known West Point credo: *I will not lie, cheat, or steal,* is easy to live up to. It is the second part that people struggle with: *nor tolerate those who do.* This implies that you will act on any knowledge of wrongdoing, a far tougher task than simply policing your own actions.

". . . all reality hinges on moral foundations . . ."

—MARTIN LUTHER KING, JR.

COIN TEMPTATION

"Let your character be above reproach, for that is the way to earn men's obedience."

—MATHIAS VON SCHULENBURG: TO MARSHAL SAXE WHEN A YOUNG OFFICER, 1709

The battalion commander ran out of the custom-made coins embossed with the battalion crest. The colonel gave those coins to soldiers and family members as a token of his appreciation. He charged each company to conduct a fundraiser to help buy more coins. He said that those coins mean more to the soldiers than an award. He apparently did not understand the promotion-point worksheet.

The pursuit of those coins can lead down a slippery slope . . .

Real Life

The battalion had no coins left and no funds to buy any. They did have a hundred coffee mugs emblazoned with the unit crest, ordered for reenlistment gifts. Those tokens of appreciation quickly sprouted "For Sale" signs and a $5 price tag.

Is the profit in dollars worth the cost in integrity and respect?

GUARD YOUR HONOR

Your honor cannot be taken from you. You must give it away.

The opportunity to damage your reputation will present itself daily. Your reaction will be carefully, though discreetly, watched and graded by your people.

Everything is life is a graded event, and there is no retest.

> "What is right is often forgotten by what is convenient."
>
> —BODIE THOENE,
> *WARSAW REQUIEM*

CRITICISM

Little steps for little feet; in other words, praise movement in the right direction.

Reward people for getting closer to the goal you set. Do not wait for a perfect product. Few people hit a home run their first time at bat. Give some recognition and reward for improvement, even a little improvement. You cannot be all stick and no carrot.

> "Any fool can criticize, condemn and complain—and most do."
>
> —DALE CARNEGIE, *HOW TO WIN FRIENDS AND INFLUENCE PEOPLE*

SUCK UP AND MOVE UP

Radio time is not face time. Get off the command net and use your own frequency.

Real Life

Face Time vs. Air Time

"Iron Six out." The speaker in the battalion operations center noted the end of the battalion commander's radio call. The NCOs on duty in the operations center smirked and began to count, "One, two, three, four." Then the radio crackled to life, "Operations

center, this is Razor Six, still enroute to the check-point." The operations center roared with laughter.

The captain known as Razor Six was reviled as an intense suck-up. His most humorous habit was following any call from the battalion commander with one of his own in hopes that the senior officer would still be monitoring his radio. His weak toadyism was so obvious he became a joke with the NCOs who monitored the radio.

ETHICS

"As many are soldiers that are not captains . . . So many are captains that are not soldiers."

—A WOMAN IN A WEATHERCOCK, 1609

A professional soldier is not what you do; it must be what you are. You can't simply talk it; you have to *live* it. Accomplish the mission ethically. Guard your honor, honesty in all things.

Real Life

Baloney Sandwiches
Two lieutenants were assisting with a field evaluation. They were not sleeping in the field that night and had not paid to eat in the field. It was the unit's tenth day in the field, and many soldiers were putting MREs directly into the trash. One lieutenant ate a discarded meal. The other foolishly did also.

Captain Steve Pinter saw what they did; so did a group of soldiers. Pinter took immediate action.

He strode over to two miscreant lieutenants, ordered them to the position of attention and proceeded to chew their butter-bar butts. He loudly proclaimed words like "integrity", "professionalism" and "honor." The senior of the two lieutenants could see junior soldiers discreetly watching; he began to sink into his boots. It was years before he realized how wise Steve Pinter was.

Captain Pinter could not allow privates to think that officers would eat their chow to avoid paying for their own. Even meals taken from the trash. The lieutenants stupidly gave the impression that integrity was situational, not an inviolate principle. A confidential rebuke would not have corrected the impression in the soldiers' minds.

A public flogging was called for and delivered.

ETHICAL PRIORITIES

Real Life

The platoon sergeant proudly gave the lieutenant a brand new Army-issue thermos. The young officer asked how many the platoon had received. He replied, "Twenty." Six men did not receive a thermos. He asked who they were. The sergeant indicated the six newest privates.

These were the men who routinely stood guard duty. They were the soldiers in need of hot coffee at midnight. The platoon leader directed the misguided sergeant to collect the thermoses and reissue them, starting with the lowest ranking soldiers.

SITUATIONAL ETHICS

"Between two evils, choose neither; between two goods, choose both."

—TRYON EDWARDS

There is no refuge when trapped between honesty and loyalty. Soldiers swear to uphold the law of the land. This infers an obligation of integrity, as in the well-known "I will not lie, cheat or steal" credo. When your boss requires situational ethics, however, you may face two appalling alternatives.

Real Life

At a battalion briefing, the company commander told the colonel that his lieutenant had responsibility for an area of company administration that had fared poorly in an inspection. The colonel looked at the junior officer, who was never assigned the duty, and asked, "When were you notified that you were the responsible officer?"

He sat in the chair with both of his superiors glaring. The captain might not be worthy of loyalty, but he was the company commander nonetheless. The lieutenant could not throw away his obligation to him, yet was unwilling to destroy his integrity with a lie.

What did he do? Nothing. He just sat there. An eternity of eye contact passed before the colonel muttered, "I thought so."

ALSO:

The same company commander had established a policy to always wear dog tags. To enforce his edict he would do "dog tag check" after PT. Soldiers without them had to low crawl a muddy strip that ran the length of the company area.

The policy was not particularly effective, although offensive and resented. Soon, large numbers of soldiers were deliberately reporting without their dog tags as a sign of contempt for the commander. The muddy low crawl was a badge of honor. The angry commander then required both the soldier and his supervisor to low crawl, a requirement that fostered even greater resentment.

Then came the day that the commander's driver had no dog tags.

The company was silent as he ordered the operations sergeant to crawl with the driver.

The captain reasoned that the soldier filled a company clerk slot, therefore the sergeant was responsible—a point of view not shared by the operations sergeant.

This thread of logic was lost on the men in formation and, of course, the operations sergeant. The commander lost much ground that morning.

You are a commander because the Army saw value in you. You are a leader because

your soldiers do. That is a powerful, yet frag-
ile, appointment. Guard it well.

*"People ask you for
criticism, but they only
want praise."*

—WILLIAM SOMERSET MAUGHAM,
OF HUMAN BONDAGE, 1915

HONESTY
Be careful what you ask for.

Real Life

*The new first sergeant asked his soldiers how well he
was doing his job. He asked every sergeant in his
unit to evaluate him on a standard NCO evaluation
report.*

*With one exception, the reports were vague and
ambiguous, allowing the senior sergeant to interpret
the answers in a favorable light. One subordinate
took the first sergeant at his word and submitted a
critical evaluation. The result was an hour at parade rest in front of a very disappointed senior NCO.*

They both learned a lesson that day.

---

*"Don't tell me how hard
you work. Tell me how
much you get done."*

—JAMES LING IN *NEWSWEEK*

EFFECTIVENESS
Only results count. You may have heard that
the road to hell is paved with good intentions; so is the road to Arlington.

Army schools grade students on their
ability to grasp doctrinal principles and
apply them to hypothetical situations. Real
units grade leaders on results. Blind adher-
ence to doctrine is not an excuse for failure.

SOLDIERS' EVALUATION OF YOU

Everything in life is a graded event. This is the single most important tenet of leadership. You are evaluated on duty and off, in the mall on Saturday or when soldiers happen to see you at the amusement park. The one time you screw up will be the only time remembered.

A good NCO once characterized a captain as: "He is every NCO's idea of an officer." Read that line again slowly, folks. It is not a compliment.

> "Be bold in what you stand for and careful what you fall for."
>
> —RUTH BOORSTIN IN *THE WALL STREET JOURNAL*

EXCUSES

You may have heard the cliché: "The maximum effective range of an excuse is zero." It's true.

An excuse is a weak attempt to avoid *personal responsibility*. Personal responsibility is an indicator of commitment to an ideal, personal courage, and trust in your leaders. Bottom line: Resist the short-term benefit of an excuse. Cling to the long-term power of personal responsibility.

> "Excuses are nails used to build a house of failure."
>
> —DON WILDER AND BILL RECHIN

CONFIDENCE IN YOURSELF

Confidence in yourself builds other's confidence in you. The confidence of others is critical to leadership.

Confidence is the sum of your professional knowledge, personal experience and

> "Trust yourself. You know more than you think you do."
>
> —BENJAMIN SPOCK, M.D.

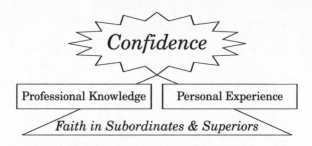

faith in you. That's a lot. Trust your instincts. Trust yourself.

COURAGE

"Courage is a special kind of knowledge: the knowledge of how to fear what ought to be feared and how not to fear what ought not to be feared."

—DAVID BEN-GURION

Your greatest challenge may not be physical courage on the battlefield, risking life and limb, but moral and ethical courage in the conference room risking disapproval and loneliness. Soldiers proudly proclaim they would die for the country, the mission, and fellow soldiers, but will not risk their evaluation reports.

There are no bugles and flags for a casualty of moral courage, no honored resting place in our national field of heroes. Perhaps there should be.

Moral courage takes many forms:

Real Life

The battalion was deployed to Fort Polk, Louisiana. Each morning in the dining facility the bored soldiers would eat breakfast while enjoying a movie on the wall-mounted TV/VCR.

The young leader was nearly finished with his meal when he realized the dining room was absolutely silent, each soldier frozen in his position. Not a word was said. Not a fork was moved. Every eye was fixed on the television. The confused young sergeant turned toward the set, and finally understood: someone had replaced the usual movie with a graphic example of the pornographer's art.

He heard plates clatter, and turned to watch several women soldiers abandon their uneaten meals and leave. The junior NCO stood and walked past several officers and senior sergeants to turn off the television. If he was expecting support from his senior leaders, he was disappointed. They booed and hissed like all the rest.

Everything in life is a graded event.

SOLDIERS

FAMILY READINESS GROUP (FRG)

Family Readiness Group: An unofficial group of family members who cooperate for mutual support, particularly when units are deployed.

The FRG is either a great blessing or a great burden. The more your unit deploys, the greater the participation in the support group and (maybe) the appreciation of it.

Volunteers run the group. They are there because they want to be. When you create an atmosphere that they do not want to be in, they stop coming. In particular, an atmosphere of rank-elitism will quickly kill participation among the very group you seek to assist: the young enlisted families. The effects of such an atmosphere will soon spread.

The spouse of an officer or senior NCO often chairs the group. The potential for at least the *appearance* of rank-elitism is great.

The FRG is often the ultimate test of leadership.

73

Nothing will destroy the good will of the group faster than the words "I want to . . . ," spoken by such a spouse or any other inference that he or she is in charge due to their spouse's position.

Real Life

The junior spouse had gone to great effort to host the family readiness group meeting. She planned an icebreaker game to help people get acquainted. The commander's spouse told her, "No games." When she asked why not, the commander's spouse casually replied, "Because I am in charge, and I said no." The goodwill and participation of the junior spouse slipped away . . . along with that of every other spouse to whom she recounted the incident.

The family readiness group is the ultimate test of leadership. Unlike soldiers, volunteers can leave at anytime. To motivate participation, the leader and the group must offer members something they cannot provide themselves.

FAMILY READINESS GROUP INFORMATION

There are three reasons people participate in Family Readiness Group: social contacts, assisted living, and information.

Spouses who participate for social reasons are often willing to provide the structure and administration of the group.

Those who join for assisted living range from newcomers who need an emergency phone number for the school nurse, to the spouse with no money, no car, no groceries, and four kids.

Those who participate for information want to know what their spouse and the unit are doing, and most importantly, when they will return. If the FRG can not provide more information than they already have, they leave the group.

Real Life

A 2:00 A.M. tent fire slightly injured two soldiers and destroyed thousands of dollars' worth of equipment. The battalion commander waited until morning to call the FRG, thousands of miles away.

When the FRG leader answered the phone, she was furious. She had received phone calls all night from frantic spouses asking, "Who was hurt?"

The battalion commander learned that soldiers will find a way to communicate, even in a distant desert. Unit family members learned that timely information wasn't available from the FSG leader.

RESPONSIBILITY
FOR SOLDIERS' HEALTH

You are responsible for the health of your people; the sick call doctor is not, the triage nurse is not, you are. If you think a soldier is too sick to work, you send them home. You call to check on them. You ensure the medical professions provide the best care possible. You are responsible.

HELP ME, I'M DRUNK

Every soldier needs a wallet-size phone roster that he or she can use to call for a ride when his or her car breaks down, or to inform the unit if he or she will return late from leave.

HIV POLICY

Know the Army HIV policy. Be prepared. Follow the rules. Do the right thing for your soldier, your unit, and your Army.

Home visitations are a delicate issue.

HOME VISITATION

Real Life

The soldier was deployed to Southwest Asia as an individual replacement. His family lived in Army housing. The chain of command called to check on his family weekly and ensured that a pair of NCOs (one male, one female) made an appointment to stop by monthly. Unfortunately, no one asked specific questions of the NCOs who made the house calls.

The MP duty officer called the company commander at midnight on Saturday. While responding to a complaint of loud and drunken behavior at the house, military police were appalled at the squalor and filth the children endured.

The house had broken windows, which allowed the winter wind to blow through. This reduced the stench of old garbage, bags of dirty diapers, and curdled baby bottles that were inside the small house. No arrests were made, but child protective services took the children.

In an effort to help the mother remain in housing and keep her children, at least until the husband returned, the platoon sergeant and a dozen volunteers spent the weekend cleaning and disinfecting the quarters.

Earlier intervention probably would have made everyone happier.

HOSPITAL VISITATION

A member of the chain of command visits every soldier in the hospital every day. This includes those at the downtown medical center.

To really impress a soldier, visit one of his or her family members in the hospital. It shows that you not only know what is happening in his or her life but also care.

SECTION VISITS

Visit soldiers on their turf. Make a standing offer to visit any section or unit to talk about anything, at the request of the leader.

Visit your soldiers on duty. Start with the smallest, most unpopular duty or tasker, especially if your people are attached to other organizations. Ask when their supervisor last checked on them. How is their chow, mail or other support getting to them? When was the last time their chain of command saw them?

Find two things right for every fault. Tell them and their supervisor about the commendable accomplishments you see, and follow it up by a letter or note.

SOLDIERS ON QUARTERS

Do you know who is sick and bedridden in their quarters or barracks room? Be careful. A thoughtless leader had a soldier sick in the barracks in a single room over the weekend. The ill soldier took a turn for the worse, far worse. No one checked on her until Monday morning and found her in a semicoma. It could have been tragic.

NICKNAMES

"Nicknames stick to people, and the most ridiculous are the most adhesive."

—THOMAS C. HALIBURTON

Be careful of the names you allow to be assigned to others. Ignore the ones that are assigned to you. You are not as good as the complementary monikers, nor as despicable as the others.

SPONSORSHIP

Every soldier and spouse is sponsored.

Each section has designated sponsors for incoming soldier by rank, job specialty, and marital status.

A sponsor should be the best you have. This is the first step in growing good soldiers. The sponsor and new soldier should be inseparable for the first few days in your unit.

You must personally check on the sponsorship program to demonstrate its importance to you.

A strong sponsor is an investment in the future.

DRINKING AT OFFICIAL FUNCTIONS

Do not drink at social functions. If you must, drink the least of everyone there, especially your seniors. A careless word or action that you may not even recall can destroy your career.

"One of the disadvantages of wine is that it makes a man mistake words for thoughts."

—SAMUEL JOHNSON

Real Life

The lieutenant's wife was drunk at the New Year's Day reception in the battalion commander's house. The battalion executive officer discreetly advised him to take his wife home. As the major turned, the fun-loving spouse slapped him soundly on top of his bald head. The entire room turned to stare. She rewarded her startled audience with an encore.

How do you measure the damage of her actions?

BLOOD ALCOHOL LEVEL

The first thing your boss will ask when he learns of a serious incident is, "Was alcohol involved?"

Following any serious accident or incident of indiscipline, take those involved to the MP station and have them tested for alcohol. If it is a serious offense, read them their rights first. This allows you to exonerate those who did not indulge in alcohol and appropriately punish those who did.

MOTIVATION
KITA

"A KITA [kick-in-the-ass] leads to movement, not motivation."

—FREDERICK HERZBERG

Sometimes, though, that is enough.

RECOGNITION

Consider Christmas or birthday cards with a note inside.

A form letter (with a personal note from you on the bottom) to your subordinates on their birthdays is effective. More effective is the same letter to their spouses on *their* birthdays, with a note on the bottom. Only a handwritten note counts; use of digital signatures, or worse—your secretary's handwriting—will generate an embarrassing nickname.

Deaths or other tragic events deserve a timely card at least. A leader who must purchase an appropriate card after the event has already failed to plan.

Once begun, however, you cannot miss anyone.

REWARDS

A key to effectively motivating people is finding the things they do well and publicly rewarding them. One platoon sergeant presented the "Play of the Week" to the week's best good deed at the last formation on Friday. The winner was entitled to a three-day pass.

Real Life

At the Thursday night meeting each squad leader submitted a great deed for consideration for the Play of the Week. When one squad leader reported he had nothing to offer, the platoon sergeant called in several members of the young NCO's squad and asked them what they would like submitted. They had several worthy items. The embarrassed squad leader never came empty-handed again.

Actively seek things done right and reward them.

Reward people in ways that encourage superior performers. If, for example, you offer to allow individual PT for anyone who scores 300 on the PT test, what incentive does that give those who can already do it? What does that offer to those who feel they can never reach it? Would a reward based on improvement in the raw score be better?

NCO WORK

"NCO work." That phase should mean intense personal involvement with individual soldier training, leading, and caring. Too often it is a shield to prevent senior leaders from checking.

A competent and proficient NCO wants people to check his work. He wants his people to be recognized for superior performance. A mediocre performer avoids inspection. He doesn't want his unsatisfactory performance discovered. His soldiers recognize his shortcomings. They wonder why you can't.

Leaders check, supervisors check, even managers check. Good performers welcome it. Poor performers fear it.

STUPID ACCIDENTS

Real Life

The Commander inspected the platoon's Bradley Fighting Vehicles late Friday afternoon. It had been a

"Any officer can get by on his sergeants. To be a sergeant you have to know your stuff. I'd rather be an outstanding sergeant than just another officer."

—GUNNERY SERGEANT DANIEL DALY

long week filled with too much work and too little sleep.

The captain was not technically competent to inspect the mechanical operation of the vehicles so he concentrated on cleanliness. The platoon had prepared with this fact in mind.

His disappointment at not finding any significant dirt was replaced with determination to find something, anything. Finally, he reached into the engine compartment, smearing his hand in grease. His frustration exploded as he delivered a loud and public ass-chewing. He then declared that no soldier would leave the motorpool until every bilge was clean, then he walked out of the motor pool.

Each squad sent a soldier for solvent to clean the bilge. One weary sergeant noticed that the gasoline pumps were closer than the solvent barrels. He filled his bucket, and dumped it into the engine compartment. Moments later a fireball erupted.

The thoughtless soldier survived only due to the automatic fire extinguishing system in the vehicle.

THE POWER OF APPRECIATION: DEEDS, NOT WORDS

Everyone admits they couldn't get promoted without the commitment of their people. Few leaders repay that commitment.

"Words are plentiful, but deeds are precious."

—LECH WALESA

Real Life

The sergeant major had the entire battalion on the parade field at 0555, standing at attention, anticipating the arrival of the battalion commander and the start of a five-mile run, followed by the usual busy day.

The battalion commander strode to the microphone and to everyone's surprise, commanded, "At ease!" He continued, "I was just informed by the brigade commander that I've been selected for promotion. We all know it wasn't my efforts that made it possible; it was yours. So after completion of the run, take the rest of the day off, on me."

ASSOCIATES

"Books, like friends, should be few and well chosen."

—SAMUEL PATERSON

It is true what your mother told you: Birds of a feather actually do flock together. People associate because of common interests or values. You can often judge a person by the company he keeps. Look at your best subordinates. They generally associate with other high-performance people. Your poor performers find much in common with other poor performers.

How do your associates reflect on you?

NEWCOMER CERTIFICATION

Use a certification program for incoming soldiers and leaders. The requirements of the program must directly impact the person's ability to perform his or her mission relative to his or her military occupational specialty (MOS) and duty assignment. Your intent is for incoming soldiers to be *successful.*

THE NEW GUY

New soldiers of any rank will hesitate to question a stupid order or refuse bad advice from a veteran. They fear their hesitation will be viewed as a sign of weakness or incompetence.

"The most consistent trait of the new guy is his refusal to ask for help, even when he is chin deep in shit and sinking fast."

—CAPT. RANDY WEST

The timeless tradition of sending the new man on an all-day quest for a can of "track tension" is a common example of using the fear of embarrassment to destroy the confidence of new soldiers.

FEAR

New members of any organization fear embarrassment above all else. That fear drives the new soldier out of the aircraft door on his first parachute jump, or over the cliff on his first repel as his new unit looks on. It's a powerful force, seldom understood, often misused, and sometimes resulting in tragedy.

Real Life

The truck platoon formed a convoy a half-mile long. The youngest and newest member of the platoon was driving the next-to-last truck.

The choking dust at the rear of the convoy reduced visibility to a few feet. The young soldier lost sight of the truck ahead. Fear of getting lost overpowered his caution. Hoping to catch up to the vehicle ahead, he quickly sped up.

A veteran manned the vehicle in front of the frantic young soldier. He did not fear getting lost; he was rightfully afraid he would accidentally hit the truck ahead. He slowed down. The impact crushed the cab of the new soldier's truck, and the young man inside.

The tragic results ended the speeding young soldier's career, and nearly his life.

RECOGNIZING AN EMERGENCY

"A leader has the ability to recognize a problem before it becomes an emergency."

—ARNOLD H. GLASGOW

If a subordinate is screaming for help, he at least has time to call. If he is too busy to talk to you on the radio he must be fighting for survival.

BARRACKS PRESENCE

What is the chain of command's responsibility in the barracks? How often do they visit the barracks? Probably not often on weekends or holidays. Check the duty NCO's log for chain of command attendance. Then tell your subordinates that you check the log. That makes it a graded event.

The best times to check day rooms, latrines, and other common areas are on weekends and holidays, particularly on long weekends.

Real Life

The platoon leader checked the barracks one holiday weekend and put a soldier on ordinary leave who was denied emergency leave to attend a funeral.

The soldier's NCO was technically correct regarding the standards for emergency leave, but the situation allowed the chain of command to do the RIGHT thing just as easily.

CHAPLAIN

A good chaplain is a critical resource for leaders. He is a conduit into the hearts and minds of soldiers. The astute commander develops and cultivates the chaplain; he encourages routine informal communication and publicly acknowledges his input.

The chaplain must demonstrate influence on the chain-of-command to gain credibility with soldiers. He must also demonstrate good judgment in the cases he pleads, to gain credibility with the command. This is particularly difficult for new chaplains. He may have little Army experience and no nearby peers for advice and counsel. He often turns to the person he spends the most time with—his young enlisted assistant.

The chaplain's assistant can provide valuable insight concerning the soldiers of the unit, but he may not recognize the complex challenges facing the commander. That responsibility belongs to the chaplain. His understandings of these issues will build or destroy his credibility with the commander.

Chaplains are soldiers, too. They must seek—and get—the commander's attention as much as the other staff officers.

BIRTHS

"Children are one-third of our population and all of our future."

—SELECT PANEL FOR THE PROMOTION OF CHILD HEALTH, 1981

Acknowledge births with a note or card to the family. You get the information from the SITREP or through the first sergeant or platoon sergeant. It is imperative that no one be missed.

Some units provide a token gift for the birth. This should be from the unit, not from an individual member of the chain of command. You must be timely. You must not miss anyone.

"HEY, YOU" DETAILS

Absolutely forbid "hey, you" details (last-minute duties assigned on the basis of who will answer their door in the barracks) unless authorized by you or your first sergeant. Require a written justification the next day.

Real Life

The food service NCO called her commander at 0100 Sunday morning. "Sir, the brigade operations officer just called and ordered me to send three of my cooks to the field in two hours, to support the commanding general's mess. What do you want me to do?"

The company commander called the brigade operations officer and explained he did not believe that three previously tasked cooks had suddenly disappeared, only that the operations officer was screwing soldiers due to the incompetence of his own staff. The company commander emphasized that if the senior officer insisted on a "hey, you" tasking, he would personally see the brigade commander under the open door policy.

The S3 decided that the additional cooks would not be needed after all.

*"Three generations in a
regiment count for less
in the eyes of our Army
Council than three
miserable marks in a
miserable competitive
examination."*

—SIR IAN HAMILTON:
THE SOUL AND BODY OF AN ARMY,
1921

PROMOTION BOARDS

You must send soldiers to the Soldier of the Month board. It is valuable practice under stressful conditions. It builds crucial confidence they will need when they face their squad, section, or platoon in a leadership position.

Boards impose a leadership test on the first-line supervisor as well. They allow both the leader and the soldier visibility with the command sergeant major and other senior leaders in the battalion. The soldier's performance reflects on his entire chain of leadership, including you.

First-line supervisors should accompany candidates to the board. If the candidate appears in his or her dress uniform (Class A uniform), so does the supervisor.

Real Life

Specialist Mack was the most unlikely candidate ever to appear before a board. He was technically proficient, but lacked the poise and depth of knowledge necessary to prevail at the Soldier of the Month board, at least his lieutenant thought so. The soldiers in the platoon were determined to overcome these disadvantages for the popular young man.

Each person in the platoon learned several questions from the battalion's study guide. Everywhere poor Mack went, someone asked him questions. His anxiety and aggravation rose as the board neared.

His victory surprised no one more than Mack himself. The experience changed him. He was more confident. It changed the platoon as well. The mutual commitment and shared sense of accomplishment built a team, where only co-workers existed before.

THE COLOR GUARD

If you provide a color guard for a formal dinner, they should eat at no charge, in a place of honor. Do not segregate them at a separate table in the back as hired help. Treat them like the honored guests they are.

Real Life

The sergeant major told the Soldier of the Month and the Soldier of the Quarter they would both be invited to the sergeants' major formal dinner. The young soldiers were flattered. They were instructed to be at the NCO Club the day prior for rehearsal.

The soldiers ensured their uniforms were perfect when they reported for rehearsal. Only then did they understand they were to be ushers. Their sergeant major did not notice their disappointment. He announced that both their meals were paid for and a table was set up in the kitchen for them. One of the soldiers responded that he had thought he was to be a guest, and his wife had purchased a new dress for just this occasion. The sergeant major pondered the new development for a moment, then replied that she could come and hand out corsages to the ladies.

The hard feelings that grow out of such a blunder never heal. What was the cost to the credibility of the sergeant major?

STANDARDS

"If all is not in order, I will hang you despite my personal high regard."

—SUVAROV 1792

Standards apply to everyone. When exceptions are made, a new standard is established.

Real Life

The Headquarters Company commander reported to the battalion commander that a key staff officer had failed the physical fitness test and his personnel file would be flagged, indicating he failed to meet the required standard. The senior officer congratulated his young subordinate on tough enforcement of standards. The colonel then directed him to remove the flag paperwork. The colonel said he would personally counsel the substandard officer and observe a retest in two weeks. Only a second failure would result in flagging.

The specialist in the personnel section shook his head as he pulled the errant officer's paperwork from a stack that included several junior soldiers who also failed the physical fitness test. These soldiers would be flagged today, although the officer would not. A new standard had been established, perhaps not in the battalion commander's mind but certainly in the perception of the clerk and the three hundred others who would know about it by the end of the week.

You can not hide a dead fish. It stinks; so does this.

You are not running for election or sainthood here. Be tough when necessary, impartial always. Guard you honor.

COMMUNICATION

VOCABULARY

Don't try to prove you were number one in your class at West Point or the only ROTC graduate at Yale. Remember to C.Y.A. (Consider Your Audience) when choosing your words.

"Think like a wise man but communicate in the language of the people."

—WILLIAM BUTLER YEATS

RUMORS

Rumor control at morning physical training: Take two minutes before the formation ends and ask for questions. There won't be any at first. Keep at it. Eventually you will be able to squash some incredible misinformation. Any issues brought to your attention anonymously via your personal voicemail or e-mail are answered here, if appropriate.

SITUATION REPORTS

This is the weekly situation report you demand from your subordinates, and provide

---

ALPHA COMPANY
SITUATION REPORT, WEEK OF 2 SEPTEMBER 2005

HIGH POINTS

Chances to point out the great things your people are doing.

More services in the field than any other company, thanks to SFC Hall and his m

Alpha gave 55% of the battalion's blood donation. Same old story.

We have 52 attendees for the dining-out so far. ISG explains it as "Doing the professional thing."

SPC McQueen and SPC Howard are doing well in PLDC.

Hail & Farewell was fabulous. Great work by Charlie Company.

LOW POINTS

Turnout at prayer breakfast was poor, especially among senior leaders. We should support the chaplain better.

Last-minute tasking for trucks for the Phantom Saber Exercise destroyed the published training schedule.

Your chance to highlight issues you need help on.

ISSUES

SPC Daniel's move to Headquarters Company: Hurts the Soldier, hurts your maintenance, and confuses priorities. Recommend I send my driver for your interview instead.

Drivers training schedule: must compress if we're to finish prior to deployment. If so, when?
Each passing day costs us graduates. I've spoken with the S3 at length; he is unwilling to flex the schedule.

TRAINING TO VISIT

Land navigation at, 0800 on 9 September. This is 2LT Jones' first platoon training exercise. Your presence would be a great motivator. I can have my HMMWV pick you up.

You have input into where your boss will show up. Great chance to get some visibility for your junior leaders. Make sure the training is rehearsed and by the book.

---

to your seniors. It should cover the good things your people have done for the week as well as difficulties or ongoing actions. Also indicate events for the boss to visit the next week. Prepare your subordinates for the visit. This is a golden opportunity for your subordinate leaders to impress the battalion commander.

Mention, by name, the good things your people have done. Post a copy of your SITREP for your people to see. They will know you give them credit for their actions.

WHEN LESS IS MORE

If you cannot speak well, but you cannot resist an opportunity to speak; if you ramble; if you spend way too long saying way too little; you may need to speak less and say more.

"He can compress the most words into the smallest idea of any man I ever met."

—ABRAHAM LINCOLN

You degrade the credibility of your good ideas by burying them in a mountain of meaningless verbiage. Less really is more.

INFORMATION FLOW

Enforce the "information through me rule." If you allow yourself to be bypassed, you will be *uninformed* and *unimportant*.

Uninformed is unimportant.

Post on the bulletin board a copy of your SITREP to your boss for your subordinate's information. This emphasizes to them that you are indeed singing their praises when they excel. Personally embarrassing information should never be posted for public consumption.

The SITREP you receive from your subordinates is how you monitor the pulse of the little guys. Insist you get them. Keep them on file.

LISTENING

If you are not listening more than talking, you are missing something important. Work hard at listening, physically, mentally, in attitude, and in appearance. It encourages people to talk.

FAREWELL TO YOUR UNIT

You demanded 100% from your soldiers every day. Expect no less of yourself when saying good-bye.

Get a roster of the entire unit and personally say thanks and good-bye to each soldier.

You must see everyone, the good and the bad. You go to their place of duty. You get extra points for seeing people one at a time rather than in groups. The larger the group you thank at a time, the less it means. If you line up your entire squad, platoon, company or battalion and give a group thanks and farewell, you get zero points.

COMMAND PHILOSOPHY

An effective command philosophy provides guidance in situations you never anticipated. The acid test of a published command philosophy is whether the most junior soldier in you unit understands it. The wise leader writes in the language of the common man.

An effective command philosophy is short, simple and memorable. Put the bottom line upfront. Can you remember the command philosophy of your last commander?

After you write it, you have to live it. You must continually demonstrate commitment to your published philosophy, or it will just be another piece of yellowed paper on the bulletin board.

CONTACT TIME

A weekly breakfast (or other neutral setting) meeting with subordinate leaders will tell you things you never suspected about your unit. Ask probing open-ended questions. Ask the thousand other things that leaders assume happen routinely but fall through the cracks at the muddy-boot level.

Contact time with your people builds insight . . . from both directions.

You will find out many things you never suspected. You will find out many things you will not like. How well you accept bad news will determine how much you'll receive in the future.

Have a meeting with outgoing soldiers. Breakfast or other meal is a neutral meeting place. Use the mess hall. Your privates can eat there cheap. Have the mess sergeant reserve tables for you. Be thick skinned so they can be candid.

If you do not spend half your time on patrol within your unit, you are missing something important somewhere.

Have departing officers and NCOs outbrief you personally. Use a standard "base" of questions to develop trends.

NEWSPAPERS

News is a precious commodity in the field. Rumors will multiply without some source of information. Newspapers, books, and magazines provided to the unit don't belong to an individual. They certainly don't belong to the command group, battalion staff, or headquarters platoon.

The better the condition the papers are in, the fewer the soldiers who have had the opportunity to read them.

FACT VS. RUMOR

Nature abhors a vacuum; so does information. Soldiers fill the information vacuum with rumor, innuendo, and supposition. This degrades morale and damages leaders' credibility.

Leaders are responsible for the flow of information to every soldier. If leaders do not check, it will not happen.

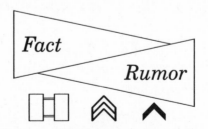

The higher the rank,
the greater the amount of factual information available

GOSSIP

Resist this great temptation. It leads to misunderstandings, anger and hurt feelings. It is difficult to say "No thanks," to gossip. Persevere. If you are strong enough to consistently decline gossip, the gossipmongers will stop offering.

"Who gossips to you will gossip about you."
—TURKISH PROVERB

WRITING

Writing is often the most common way to communicate with your seniors. Your words portray an image of you that can be far-reaching and long lasting. Once, a young officer was selected as the interim battalion S3 because the report of survey he completed was properly formatted and well written. That selection changed his career and his life.

"It is a damned poor mind indeed that can't think of at least two ways to spell any word."
—ANDREW JACKSON, QUOTED BY WILLIAM SAFIRE IN *QUOTH THE MAVEN*

The policy letters, counseling, evaluation reports and everything else you write communicates with your subordinates. What you say is only part of the communication. Format, clarity, spelling and grammar also send a message.

What impression do yours give?

COMMUNICATION IS THE KEY TO COMMAND

Communication is the foundation of all relationships. Everything is communication.

Communication is the key to command. Communication is far more than what you

Leadership is a relationship. All relationships are built on communication.

say or write. It is what you wear, how you walk and talk, your demeanor and bearing, how your uniform looks, and a thousand other details that you take for granted but which your soldiers evaluate every day.

Use a suggestion box. Better yet, a voice mailbox. It allows calls at any hour, and soldiers are not afraid you might actually answer the phone in the middle of the night on an ordinary answering machine. Answer anonymous questions by stating the questions and answers publicly following the physical fitness formation. If the soldier wants a personal reply he must include his name.

ROLODEX™

Your Rolodex (or electronic address book) is a powerful tool. You load it with ammunition by the names and offices and numbers you put in it. Include personal and professional information when appropriate.

THE DANGER OF E-MAIL

You control only the first recipient of your e-mail.

E-mail is a dangerous thing when combined with a short temper, and a colorful vocabulary. The sender controls only the first people the message will reach, not the last. The ill-advised correspondence may be copied, forwarded, and posted far beyond the intended audience.

Real Life

The brigade commander fired an angry memo to all his battalion commanders. The logic of the message was ridiculous. The language was unsavory and the grammar and punctuation laughable. Displaying even less forethought, the battalion commanders promptly forwarded the embarrassing e-mail to all company commanders. The company grade officers, the object of the brigade commander's fury, found the mail amusing and forwarded copies to their acquaintances Army-wide.

An angry memo, which would never have left brigade headquarters if the colonel had to dictate it, proof it and sign it, traveled the world in a few days.

E-MAIL: EVERYTHING IN LIFE IS A GRADED EVENT

Half of all e-mail is jokes, endlessly forwarded from one person to another. Beware: What you deem valuable or humorous enough to forward is a reflection on you. Stories of a sexual, racial, or derogatory nature forwarded by you are construed as an indicator of your own standards, values, and character.

Jokes you don't approve, of, but are forwarded with your name on the addressee

> *"Nothing shows a man's character more than what he laughs at."*
>
> —JOHANN WOLFGANG VON GOETHE

list, also reflect on you. Get your name off those lists.

SITUATION REPORT
Are you getting copies of all subordinates' SITREPs? If not, you are being left out of the communication loop. You will be uninformed and possibly embarrassed one day.

COUNSELING

THE KEY TO COUNSELING

The key to counseling is regularity and detail.

Counseling is a record of expectations and achievements.

Regularity:

Counsel often. It's better to acknowledge great achievements, and encourage continued superior performance, monthly than quarterly. It is certainly better to counsel substandard performance monthly, than quarterly.

Regularly scheduled counseling provides a systematic framework for developing and checking goals and objectives.

Details:

Use hard data first, such as dates, numbers, percentages and other objective criteria of performance. This lends credible support to your subjective assessment of performance and demonstrates that you see and grade daily accomplishments.

> *"He that won't be counseled can't be helped."*
> —BENJAMIN FRANKLIN

Clearly define objectives with timeline and standards. Measure performance against last month's assigned objectives. That is the standard he or she has held himself or herself to for the period. That is how you measure success

Truly successful counseling means the soldier counsels himself or herself. The soldier provides counseling input about what he or she feels are his or her areas for improvement, what the soldier plans to do about them, and when and how he or she expects to show results. In other words, he or she has committed himself or herself emotionally, not just signed the form to get you off his or her back.

Who would not want detailed performance counseling?

Real Life

The senior NCO was adamant. The only form used for counseling was the official Army NCO counseling form. Only the single small block on the form could document each three-month period. No additional sheets authorized.

This insistence had nothing to do with proper reverence for official paperwork and everything to do with his or her miserable performance.

If someone works for you for three months, they deserve more recognition, good or bad, than you can fit into four square inches on a form. This is another reason why monthly counseling is better than quarterly.

COUNSELING JOURNAL
A daily journal is invaluable for producing good counseling. It records the facts, figures, and events for your monthly counseling.

COUNSELING FORMAT
NCO counseling should mirror the categories on the back of the NCO Evaluation Report. Each category should address significant events that took place during the period, status of goals from last period, and goals for the next period. This makes annual NCOER writing relatively painless.

COUNSELING FOR ADVERSE ACTION
It is vital to counsel promptly *on paper* any soldier who is not recommended for school or promotion or receives an adverse action. This must document why he or she received the action and what he or she must demonstrate to overcome the shortcoming. The

written counseling is an important link in the chain if poor performance leads to early discharge proceedings.

FOOTLOCKER COUNSELING

Soldiers assess your reaction to unwelcome news and tailor their candor to match.

Footlocker counseling (informal discussion in a relaxed atmosphere) educates you as much as the soldier. A relaxed setting encourages soldiers to speak frankly.

After gaining their confidence you may hear things you disagree with. Be careful. Soldiers assess your reaction to unwelcome news and tailor their candor to match.

IMPACT COUNSELING

Immediate recognition of good performance is twice as valuable as punishing bad performance.

Impact counseling is the immediate written and verbal recognition of outstanding performance. Supervisors are quick to punish poor performance in this way, but real leaders do it for good performance.

Impact counseling is worth twice what periodic is. Immediate recognition of *good* performance is twice as valuable as recognizing bad.

Carry blank counseling forms. Use them to recognize great deeds. Your single sheet of paper will be the first *positive* impact counseling most soldiers will have ever seen.

If you observe truly noteworthy achievements (measured against the difficulty of the task or situation and the rank/experience of the soldier), follow up with a simple note to his or her commander through the chain of command.

INITIAL COUNSELING

Conduct regularly scheduled initial counseling for all new soldiers.

Junior soldiers may be counseled as a group. Each soldier receives a preprinted copy of the counseling form with your signature. After he or she signs, it is placed in his or her personnel file.

Initial counseling must outline your expectations of soldiers, which center on general behavior and standards; that is, to be at the right place, the right time, in right uniform and follow instructions. Leaders require more specific and extensive counseling.

COUNSELING FILE CONTENTS

Using an officer's OER support form is a good idea for your senior NCOs. You expect your senior leaders to perform based on goals and objectives rather than procedures. The support form makes them obligate themselves to definable goals.

Put a promotion point worksheet in every E1 through E5 counseling packet. It shows soldiers where they will stand once they reach E4 and let you evaluate what junior noncommissioned officers have done recently to advance themselves.

PERSONAL COUNSELING

You cannot solve other people's personal problems. They must solve their own. Be a good listener. Direct with guiding questions. Refer to professionals as appropriate. The soldier must come to his or her own conclusion.

PLATE COUNSELING

A fancy name for a simple (and informative) act of comradeship.

This is a fancy name for sharing a meal with your subordinates. Conducted on a one-on-one basis. Whether you go to Burger King or sit in your Hummer, the atmosphere should be informal and confidential. It's the same as footlocker counseling.

WHEN TO CHECK COUNSELING

Check the counseling packets of all soldiers selected for monthly random urinalysis. This gives a regular, random look at a cross section of your company, platoon, or section.

ADMINISTRATION AND MANAGEMENT

WEIGHT CONTROL PROGRAM

How will you enforce the "look's fat *is* fat" rule in AR 600-9? Who is just a little over the limit? Who is just under it? Can you justify your selection for enforcement in court?

PASSES

A logbook of all passes provides a record of who was rewarded, when, and why. This is important when a soldier asks why someone else gets all the passes. His or her perception is that the other guy got many passes. Whether this perception of favoritism is actually true or not, *he or she believes it; therefore it is true, to him or her.*

A pass logbook will either change his mind or prove she's right.

UNIFORM INSPECTIONS

The toughest part of class A uniform inspections is not inspecting the uniforms; it's the drill and ceremony required to conduct the inspection. The official Army manual doesn't provide every needed command. When in doubt, check with a senior NCO.

Real Life

The commander and first sergeant moved through the lines of soldiers, checking each uniform in turn. Determined to be thorough, the young officer firmly lifted the front of every soldier's jacket to check the shine on the brass belt buckle. Then he came to a female soldier.

He was determined to maintain the same standard for male and female soldiers, but reluctant to put his hands on the woman's uniform. He just stood there, stupidly.

The first sergeant allowed sufficient time to pass for the lesson to sink in, then barked, "Show the commander your belt buckle!" The young woman smartly lifted her jacket, revealing a shimmering golden buckle.

THE HEADQUARTERS PROBLEM

Headquarters is a doomsday machine. It is unstoppable and consumes everything in front of it. Its preferred fodder is a soldier from your company. Its bloated manning is hidden by a personnel report shell game.

The problem is your colonel. The brigade commander grades him on (among other things) mundane benchmarks like OER/NCOER submission time, award submissions, and a thousand other things that kill trees or burn up computers. Headquarters produces those tree-killing products. If they cannot do it on time, it must be due to insufficient people. So he or she gives them more . . . and more . . . and more.

You can fight back by sending only your worst people to fill the inevitable tasking to "reinforce failure" in the staff. This feels good in the short term, but you will soon be tasked for more people and your soldiers will suffer in the interim.

You may have heard that there is nothing more dangerous than a second lieutenant with a compass. That is not true. An incompetent staff weenie with a computer can cause far more pain. Do not send incompetent people, but rather, practice damage control. Send a reasonable performer with an understood limit to his or her tenure on the staff.

IN-BOX SHUFFLE

The "Do—Dump—Delegate" System.

Nothing goes into the commander's in-box until the first sergeant has seen it. This sensible and effective policy is only possible with the cooperation of the commander.

All actions in your in-box can be divided into three piles: Do, Dump or Delegate. Careful sorting is a time multiplier for you.

Real Life

The assistant battalion S3 placed a memo in her boss's in-basket; who promptly dropped it in the trash. The lieutenant retrieved it and announced that this memo required a reply. The senior officer casually noted: "I have received and discarded that same memo for months; no one has ever called me to ask for it. Therefore it is not important and not worthy of our time."

It's an interesting story, but a dangerous technique; use with caution.

THE PAIN OF GREAT IDEAS

"When the general lays on unnecessary projects, everyone is fatigued."

—CH'EN HAO

All projects need a "good idea" cut-off point.

Real Life

It had been a very busy first year in command, the colonel reminded his key leaders. As he continued to review the many new initiatives, programs, and requirements he had demanded during the past twelve months, everyone wondered what the next year would bring.

*The colonel finished his review with congratulations and gratitude for work well done, paused, and said, "There is only one new project for the next year." The last briefing slide flashed onto the screen: **"Hold on to what we've got."***

PROMOTION PREPARATION

A promising soldier with a GT score below 100 must attend basic educational skill training and retest satisfactorily if he or she is to be eligible for promotion.

Good leaders will stop by the classroom, observe the soldier and make sure he or she sees them. They will speak to the instructor about his or her progress.

Use the computerized personnel data card system to print a list of names in GT score order. Base your selection for the coveted basic educational skills classes on merit, not the arbitrary guides of time-in-grade, time-in-service or present GT score. The intent is to ensure the successful retention and promotion of the best young soldiers.

"There are no secrets to success. It is the result of preparation, hard work, and learning from failure."

—GEN. COLIN POWELL IN
THE BLACK COLLEGIAN

PROMOTION SELECTION

"Personnel selection is decisive. People are our most valuable capital."

—JOSEPH STALIN (FROM HARVARD BUSINESS REVIEW SEPT-OCT 88)

How are soldiers selected for waiver for early promotion?

Real Life

Two privates were eligible for early promotion to private first class. Their commander based her selection on their duty performance, as documented in their counseling files. One counseling folder described a superior soldier. The other held only an initial counseling form, which was not even written by her supervisor. Guess who was promoted early?

The soldier with the empty counseling packet was failed by her entire chain of command, from her squad leader through the company commander herself. This shouldn't happen.

WILLS

"Your son, my lord, has paid a soldier's debt."

—SHAKESPEARE, *Macbeth*

Counsel all soldiers on the need for a will.

You cannot (unfortunately) order your soldiers to get a will. You can require those who decline the opportunity to personally explain to you why they do not need it. Notice how many of those "no-will" people line up in front of the legal clerk for a will prior to a deployment.

Pressuring soldiers to get a will often generates complaints from the legal office. They contend a young soldier with no dependents needs no will. They will explain that the law already provides the means to settle a simple estate. Baloney; make the legal department do its job. Ask the attorneys if they can foresee any situation where a will would not assist the family of a young single soldier. They'll answer, "Yes, but that is a rare case." Remind the errant officer that is why each of your soldiers will be coming by for a will.

Your sacred obligation is to soldiers and their families, not the workload at the Judge Advocate General's office.

KEYBOARD TIME

Leaders' time used for typing or e-mail is not the best first use of their most precious asset. It is a great excuse not to be on patrol within your unit in foul weather, though. E-mail can tyrannize leaders' time. Use official e-mail judiciously, and not in lieu of regular face-to-face meetings with your subordinates.

Avoid the tyranny of e-mail.

CONTINUITY FILE

All leaders should have an up-to-date continuity file for their successor. They will not unless you ask to see it. By the way, do *you* have one?

If you don't ask, they won't have one.

ADDITIONAL DUTIES

Additional duties are those resented but necessary responsibilities, not assigned to a specific individual. They must be assigned fairly and impartially.

Few officers can understand the complexities of the official Army worksheet that is used to assign additional duties (DA Form 6). Wise officers seek out a respected NCO, learn the procedure and check the system. Even the computerized system is only as good as the data input. Check the data.

An officer or NCO, who incorrectly assigns duty due to his or her mistake, should personally serve the misassigned duty. This avoids screwing another soldier at the last minute due to a staff error, and ensures the staff officer will check the roster more carefully in the future.

Real Life

The brigade staff officer called Alpha Company late Friday afternoon. The officer shamelessly admitted failing to assign responsibility for a community service display the following day. Alpha Company would have to provide the detail, he declared. The Alpha commander pressed the "hold" button.

With the miscreant officer on hold, the company commander called his battalion commander, who called the brigade operations officer, who walked down the hall to educate his bungling subordinate, still foolishly holding the telephone.

When the Alpha Company commander returned to the original call, all he heard was a dial tone.

The dim-witted staff officer did a fine job at the community service display, and he never fumbled another tasking.

CUP AND FLOWER FUND

This fund, which provides its members flowers during times of grief, cups for new babies, and farewell gifts for departing members, generates immense complaining and whining. The higher the wages of the members, the more they grumble over the modest monthly dues.

No one likes the way it works, but no one volunteers to assume the administrative burden. The fund custodian, usually the unit personnel officer (S1), retains the funds until needed. The money is nonrefundable. A periodic meeting adjusts the dues to maintain an appropriate reserve, and no more.

"When a fellow says it ain't the money, but the principle of the thing, it's the money."

—KEN HUBBARD

AWARDS: DOING THE RIGHT THING

This job isn't done once an award is submitted. Leaders must check the award's status to ensure soldiers get what they deserve. Everyone should leave with his or her perfor-

mance evaluation in one hand and an award
(if appropriate) in the other.

Real Life

*The battalion personnel officer (S1) had the award
requests: for two soldiers recommended for Army
Commendation Medals (ARCOMs) from the big
field exercise. The company commander was satisfied
she had fulfilled her obligation by correctly submit-
ting the recommendations.*

*The monthly awards ceremony followed several
weeks later, but there were no awards for the two heroes. The company commander angrily confronted
the S1, who admitted that he had lost the award recommendation.*

*The award requests were reconstructed and resub-
mitted. A day later they were approved by the battalion commander . . . as Army Achievement Medals, a
lower award, because the battalion commander could
approve an Army Achievement Medal, but the
brigade commander would have had to approve the
requested Army Commendation Medals.*

Did the battalion commander down-
grade the award to avoid informing the
brigade commander of his staff's thoughtless
mistake—a mistake that might also reflect
poorly on the battalion commander himself?

IMPACT AWARDS

An impact award is by far the most effective award you can give. It must be deserved; it must be proportional to the deed; it must be public; and, above all, it must be prompt.

"Swift gratitude is the sweetest."

—GREEK PROVERB

Real Life

The battalion commander approved an Army Achievement Medal for a soldier selected as an honor graduate at a Primary Leadership Development Course (PLDC). The battalion commander pinned the award on him during the graduation ceremony, in front of his squad members and family. That was impact.

When was the last impact award presented in your unit? Look for someone *legitimate* to reward. Then make it happen *now.*

PLAY OF THE WEEK AWARD

Award the "Play of the Week" for particularly good performance. Publicize the winner, and award the soldier with a pass.

Ensure the winner actually uses the pass. If he or she is "discouraged" from using the pass by his or her supervisors, then the award will have no impact, and no interest, and you will look foolish and out of touch for presenting it.

PERSONAL EMERGENCY

Who will receive, safeguard, and deliver bad news to your soldiers? Never report a Red Cross message with devastating news over the phone or, worse yet, the radio.

Your first sergeant, operations NCO, and his or her crew must know your intent, and have a plan to implement it.

PUNISHMENT

Guide to Punishment:
Immediate—
Impartial—Public—
Proportional

Punishment should be like a hot stove: immediate, impartial, public, proportional.

Soldiers facing a UCMJ Article 15 charge must be prepared for immediate punishment. Extra duty begins as soon as the soldier leaves the commander's office. Restriction to the barracks begins that very night. Pay forfeiture documents are submitted without delay. Single parents and soldiers living off post should have their uniforms and personal hygiene supplies available in case they are punished with restriction.

The determination of guilt and administration of punishment must be absolutely impartial. The commander and the soldier's chain-of-command are being judged, even as they judge the soldier. A closed door will not prevent the entire unit from eventually knowing everything that happened.

Real Life

The tall sergeant had left Fort Irwin's dusty maintenance area against his commander's orders. Now he stood in the feeble shade of a sweltering Army tent awaiting punishment.

The commander heard the sergeant's story of good intentions overpowered by bad judgment, and then asked the first sergeant what he recommended as punishment. The commander knew the first sergeant respected the younger man; so did the youthful sergeant. The senior NCO paused, then stated, "Restriction, forfeiture of pay, and extra duty, sir; max him out."

Punishment must be public to serve as a deterrent. This doesn't mean using personal embarrassment as punishment, although embarrassment may be a consequence of misdeeds. Every soldier in the unit will soon know the rumors of what happened.

The punishment must be proportional to the crime and the perpetrator. There is no "standard punishment," although some weak and thoughtless commanders believe so. The commander's ability to wisely match the punishment to the soldier and the misdeed will be evaluated by every soldier in the unit.

> "Disgrace does not consist in the punishment but in the crime."
>
> —*VITTORIO ALFIERI*

JUSTICE AND MERCY

". . . [Punishment] is not what a lawyer tells me I may do; but what humanity, reason and justice tell me I ought to."

—EDMUND BURKE, 1775

Soldiers will stand before you for consideration of punishment. They all say they want justice. Most want their fair share of mercy, too.

Real Life

Mercy is Part of Justice

The young private was late to formation three times in two weeks. Her supervisor referred her to the company commander for punishment.

Her entire chain-of-command stood with her in the commander's office as she explained. "I'm a single mom. My baby was sick. I took him to the emergency room this morning, but forgot to call my squad leader."

The commander considered her words, then asked each of her leaders what punishment they recommended. In each case they stated, "She knew the standard. She had been warned. I recommend the maximum punishment." Finally the officer asked the trembling private, "What do you recommend?" She meekly replied, "I was wrong. I deserve to be punished. I agree with my chain-of-command, sir."

The captain paused, then stated flatly, "I agree with the chain-of-command also. I'm going to max you out, restriction, extra duty, pay forfeiture, you'll get it all."

Silence hung in the sultry heat of the small office. The petite woman was visibly shaking, struggling against tears. Her leaders were horrified. This was far more than they thought would ever be handed down, despite their recommendations.

The commander did not dismiss the shocked soldier. A minute crept by, then he asked her, "What is the purpose of punishment?" Her quivering lips couldn't speak, so he continued, "Punishment is to make people recognize an error, and correct it. Your recommendation of punishment tells me you've already done that." Again he paused, then declared, "Punishment is suspended for thirty days. Dismissed."

PUBLIC EXPOSURE

Who is responsible for getting PAO coverage for your unit? The post newspaper welcomes stories, and they love photos.

> "Everything you do or say is public relations."
> —AUTHOR UNKNOWN

A motivated young soldier with a bit of guidance and a basic grasp of grammar can get at least one story a month in the paper. The newspaper staff will go to extremes to assist. They want the story as badly as you do.

REQUIREMENTS
FOR PROJECT SUCCESS

A project must have a:
- Clear goal.
- Standards to measure achievement of that goal.
- A single hero with clearly assigned responsibility.

> "Don't undertake a project unless it is manifestly important and nearly impossible."
> —EDWIN H. LAND

- Established milestones where timeline and achievement are measured and corrective action taken.

SUPPORT FOR PROGRAMS

The big boss must publicly support your programs. Without the perception that he is using it as a measuring tool, it will have no priority. It must be tied to his rewards and sanctions.

STATISTICS

"Statistics are no substitute for judgment."
—HENRY CLAY

Leadership by statistics is the refuge of cowards. It is an insidious disease that creeps in when real discriminators, such as leadership or tactical prowess are not important or measurable.

That said, it's a pretty common way for senior raters to sort out their subordinates' evaluation reports. Plan accordingly.

RECORDS

Keep a copy of every important piece of correspondence that leaves your company.

The counseling file accompanies all Article 15 recommendations. If you don't keep a copy of the file, you will be sorry one day, and short a counseling file.

Use a sign-out sheet for anything that leaves the file cabinet. Assign responsibility for the order and maintenance of the files to one person.

SYSTEMS

The effective leader views each operation as part of a greater whole. Each task is considered as a part of a *system* to achieve the mission. If it is not part of a system to attain a defined goal, why are resources being wasted on the task?

Leaders maximize their most precious asset, personal time, by managing systems, not events. Leaders plan, resource, direct, and check other people's progress. The leader is not a worker bee, *unless his physical contribution will make the critical difference.* If that is always the case, the leader had a crummy plan to begin with.

> "If you cannot describe what you are doing as a process, you don't know what you're doing."
>
> —W. EDWARDS DEMING

MORE ON ADDITIONAL DUTIES

Soldiers are often assigned "additional duties." Lieutenants are most vulnerable to such assignments, which range from ammunition officer to voting officer. These are important duties, not to be sloughed off. Most require periodic reports and are subject to IG review.

Each additional duty is tied to an Army regulation or field manual. Ensure that you, and the persons assigned the duty, know what they are doing. Conduct periodic briefings and inspections. These test the assignees' knowledge of the subject and assure you that the duties are being properly performed.

> Additional Duties: A routine thing that can get you a severe spanking.

DISCIPLINE DRIVES ROUTINE

> "True military discipline stems not from knowledge but from habit."
>
> —GENERAL HANS VON SEECKT

Discipline makes routine things happen routinely. Leaders strive to make such ordinary events habitual. The less involvement leaders have with the ordinary, the more time and energy they can devote to the extraordinary.

FIELD MAIL

Mail is a critical aspect of morale when deployed. Mail a letter to yourself on the first and second day of the field problem. If you have not gotten them in a few days, find the problem.

MAPS

> "While the battles the British fight may differ in the widest possible ways, they have invariably two common characteristics—they are always fought uphill and always at the juncture of two or more map sheets."
>
> —FIELD MARSHAL SIR WILLIAM SLIM, UNOFFICIAL HISTORY, 1959

All leaders need a current map.

Key leaders have little time for copying current graphics and battle tracking information. Their drivers must accomplish this critical task. The driver keeps the map, SOI (code book) and vehicle ready to go at a moment's notice.

Real Life

The company commander gravely watched the OPFOR map symbols advance on his own. He reluctantly ordered his platoon leader to evacuate critical logistical supplies and equipment. He was almost too late.

The sound of gunfire engulfed the northern perimeter as the platoon leader ran to his sector screaming, "Mount up." His small column escaped over a nearby hilltop as the enemy tanks destroyed the company command post (CP).

The lieutenant's satisfaction at saving at least some assets to support the next battle evaporated when he realized he was blind and speechless. He had only the battalion and company frequencies on his radio, and his map had none of the enemy positions and persistent chemical strike graphics he so recently studied in the CP.

MEETINGS

Meetings start on time no matter what. If necessary, the senior person present presides or cancels.

> "Meetings are indispensable when you don't want to do anything."
> —JOHN KENNETH GALBRAITH

Minutes are published TODAY with appropriate actions assigned to the responsible person, as decided in the meeting. The senior person at the meeting signs the minutes. A hand written copy to each participant today is better than a typed copy tomorrow. Publish an agenda for meetings NLT the day before. Follow it. Announce the stop time of meetings in the opening remarks. Stick to it.

Real Life

The company's Wednesday afternoon training meeting had been cancelled three times due to unscheduled, but mandatory, meetings called by the battalion commander. The exasperated company commander rescheduled the training meeting at 0500 each Wednesday morning. No more "meeting conflict."

The commanding general decreed that every battalion commander would attend only one company training meeting each week. The company was ordered to move the meeting back to the convenience of Wednesday afternoon. The perpetual conflict with impromptu meetings called by the battalion commander resumed. The company commander finally understood the priorities of the battalion commander. Not respected, but understood.

Real Life

Completing the Agenda

Meetings can be time consuming, especially if there are participants who like to hear themselves talk. A senior officer chaired a working group to design a field exercise that was to test many different activities. He knew that all attendees had events and incidents to recommend to test their specialties' effectiveness, so all had to speak in turn.

To control the "talkers" he announced: "Ladies and gentlemen, we have 300 events and incidents to incorporate into this exercise plan. Everyone will be heard. If we do this efficiently and follow the agenda, we will finish at 1630. If we wander off into rhetoric or philosophy, we will not finish by 1630. In any case, we will not leave until all items on the agenda have been addressed and agreed."

It is amazing how announcing the rules of the meeting sped up completion of the working group's agenda.

MAINTENANCE
AND
TRAINING

PMCS
Preventive Maintenance Checks
and Services

When time is short, smart operators know what to check first, trouble is . . . the dumb operators think they know too.

Real Life

The eager young lieutenant was determined to demonstrate his maintenance expertise to his new platoon during the inspection. He had studied the Bradley Fighting Vehicle's maintenance manual, poring over every required check, memorizing the detailed requirements.

Unfortunately, he could find no fault on the fighting vehicles that had not been checked, and corrected. In frustration he recalled the last required check in the manual, the humidity indicator.

He was delighted to find every humidity indicator dark blue in color. It was obvious the expired chemicals, which protect sensitive electronics from moisture, had not recently been checked.

In accordance with the manual he declared all four Bradleys deadlined, or unfit for use, until the humidity indicators were replaced. He smugly turned to his sergeants and ordered, "Go get new humidity packs."

He wasn't smiling when he learned the parts were out of stock, and not expected for several weeks. Neither was his boss.

MAINTENANCE SCHEDULE

What is the maintenance schedule for your equipment? (Load tests for hoists or stands, forklift maintenance, instrument calibration, etc.). Who monitors that for you? Do your subordinate leaders, who own the equipment, brief you? Do they know the service dates? Use a standardized maintenance meeting slide.

Standard slides for your company maintenance meeting should mirror those you brief at the battalion meeting.

MAINTENANCE STANDARDS

"Another flaw in the human character . . . is that everybody wants to build and nobody wants to do maintenance."

—KURT VONNEGUT, *HOCUS POCUS*

When establishing your maintenance standards, conduct the first Friday inspections early. This allows soldiers and subordinate leaders to learn the required standards and gives them time to correct them with a full crew before quitting time.

The next Friday inspection, release the soldiers and walk the vehicle line with the platoon leaders and NCOs. Then correct deficiencies. That reinforces responsibility.

The third Friday release the entire unit. You walk the line after everyone has left. Call any deficiencies to the attention of the responsible NCO/officer for his or her personal correction before joining you (in uniform) for a 0800 Saturday morning reinspection.

Identified and quantified goals maximize motivation.

Plant your guidon at the motor pool during maintenance. The guidon stays put. You do not. Be everywhere. See everyone. Be *seen by* everyone. Stop and ask questions. Get dirty. Check for proper manuals.

Maintenance must be blocked out on the training schedule. However, more time allotted does not necessarily mean the greater benefit. Identifiable, quantifiable, graded goals maximize motivation and efficiency.

EQUIPMENT SERVICE SCHEDULE

Weapons and night vision devices should be on the service schedule. Your night vision devices require some specialized periodic inspections. If you are not checking it, who is? Do not wait for the Army Regulation (AR) 15-6 investigation. Check now.

WEAPONS MAINTENANCE

Real Life

The new first sergeant was appalled, as he stared at the lieutenant's pistol. Struggling to contain his anger, he snapped, "Sir, why is your weapon wrapped in plastic?" The new officer began to explain that since his pistol wouldn't be used during the field training exercise, there was no point in allowing it to get dirty, but a glance at the growing contempt in the NCO's face halted him. The sergeant walked away, satisfied that the lesson had been delivered, but disappointed that it was needed.

A smile crept across his face as he thought, only an officer would do something like that. He did not know the entire mortar platoon had vacuum-packed their M-16 rifles with a shrink-wrap machine.

NO PAY DUE PAY STUB

Be alert to when a soldier gets a "no-pay-due" pay voucher, and also ensure soldiers do not lose leave. Even indispensable leaders must take it.

A no-pay-due paycheck is an emergency that requires immediate action. Whatever it takes, the day cannot end until the problem is solved.

TECHNICAL COMPETENCE

You are not expected to know every facet of every soldier's job. You must, however, know enough about operations, procedures, and regulations to understand the capabilities and limitations of your soldiers and their equipment. If you do not, then you must learn.

Beware: If you try to pretend you are knowledgeable, you will be found out. Your soldiers will privately ridicule you. Your ill-considered attempt to deceive soldiers will be recalled with each decision you make.

"Real knowledge is to know the extent of one's ignorance."

—CONFUCIUS

TRAINING STANDARDS

Real Life

It was planned to be focused, diligent training on the basics of field operations. Its execution made it a joke. The long list of classes, training exercises, and rehearsals was simply added to the existing training schedule. The list of additional requirements was published on the Monday morning of Execution Week, with the admonition: "Shut up and make it happen." Each day that passed found fewer people actually attending the additional training.

Your example actually does mean something. In the above case, "maximum participation" was required at the extra classes. The battalion staff, however, could not spare time to attend such professional education. That did not stop the butt chewing of the subordinate companies for not supporting the program, though.

The battalion commander's mixed message of what really was his priority left two possibilities, neither of which was good: either he or she did not know what was really happening at the soldier level, or he or she did not care as long as he or she looked good to his boss.

RETRAINING

Retraining is used to educate a soldier, not to punish an offender.

Assigning an essay on a topic related to the error is an effective retraining tool. For example, a 1,000-word essay on the Army uniform regulation (AR 670-1) could be assigned for repeated uniform violations.

The wise leader doesn't grade such essays. He comments in green ink and returns them to the author, proving that they were actually read. His comments are charitable and positive.

Real Life

The commander's policy was clear: local laws and Army regulations required seatbelt use. Violation would write a 1,000-word essay on safety both as atonement and a learning tool.

The senior NCO was pulling out of the company parking lot when the captain stopped her. He pointed out that her shoulder belt was not in place. She owed the 1,000 words, he said. She glibly replied, "I have my belt on; I just put the shoulder harness behind me." He admitted she was absolutely correct, adding, "OK, it is only 500 words."

INTERNAL TRAINING CLASSES

Assign classes beginning with the most senior leader. If he is going to evaluate his subordinates he must demonstrate his own proficiency first. Your NCO will build or damage his reputation by his conduct in front of the troops, do him a favor; require thorough preparation.

Instructors must know upfront that their performance will be part of their monthly counseling.

Training and classes are by the book. You or a senior NCO hears the class before soldiers hear it. Encourage the use of training aids and above all, PRACTICE.

"In no other profession are the penalties for employing untrained personnel so appalling or so irrevocable as in the military."

—GEN. DOUGLAS MACARTHUR,
1933 *ANNUAL REPORT OF THE CHIEF OF STAFF.*

Invite your boss to visit your training. Offer to send your Hummer to drive him or her to your training event. Ten-minute exposure to your tough realistic training is worth two hours of PowerPoint slides in the conference room.

JUNIOR LEADERSHIP DEVELOPMENT

Junior leader training should prepare soldiers for attendance at the Primary Leadership Development Course (PLDC), which is required for promotion to sergeant.

Maintain training focus! Don't teach battlespace management or theater medical support. These soldiers will soon have to read a map, operate a radio, and put steel on target with a variety of weapons. Prepare them now. Tomorrow may be too late.

TRAINING CHALLENGE AND UNIT GROWTH

"We grow because we struggle, we learn and overcome."

—R. C. ALLEN

Nothing is static. Organizations are either growing or declining. So are the individuals within them. Challenge and change spur growth. Decline is the result of either too much or too little change.

Growth thrives on overcoming challenge. Effective leadership is motivating people to give 10% more effort than they

ORGANIZATIONAL EFFECTIVENESS

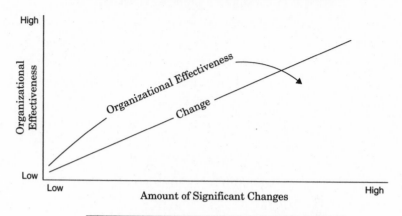

Some challenge or change is good. Too much is too much.
How much is too much depends on the leader, the situation,
the unit, and the followers.

believe they have, to achieve goals they think they can't.

Each success broadens the unit's self-perception of what it can accomplish. A wise leader provides attainable goals that soldiers feel are beyond their reach, then forces the unit to achieve those goals. The unit's confidence in themselves grows. Confidence in their leader soars.

Units with a history of doing the impossible, and doing it well, grow with each new challenge until they feel they can accomplish anything. Decline begins when they discover they cannot.

When a high performance unit meets an unattainable goal, they attack the problem with confidence and arrogance. When they realize that they will fail, they lose the cocky confidence that has served them so well in the past. They may begin to doubt. They *could* begin to decline if leaders do not find another avenue for confidence-building. It's like a professional golfer making one bad shot, but rebounding on the next.

JUDGMENT
You want subordinates with good judgment? Remember: Mistakes build experience; experience builds judgment. If you want the latter, you must accept the former.

PHYSICAL TRAINING

Never conduct a separate PT test for leaders.

An additional monthly physical training (PT) session for leaders is valuable. Rotate responsibility among sections. Give extra credit for innovation, such as a fitness trail or aerobics. This does not replace scheduled PT with soldiers.

TRAINING MOTIVATION
Leaders must set the example. Unit physical training is a *public performance* for leaders. Every eye will evaluate the leaders. The more senior the leader, the more critical the evaluation. Leaders cannot expect 100% out of

soldiers if they do not demand it of themselves. For a respected leader, soldiers may give more than they are actually capable of.

Do not allow soldiers to go on pass or other privileges if they have not passed the PT test. This is a powerful motivator for most soldiers.

Do not withhold leave. Leave is an earned benefit, not a privilege.

Real Life

The executive officer urged and intimidated a disheartened runner on the company physical fitness test who promptly collapsed after crossing the finish line. He was rushed to the hospital with severe chest pain. He recovered. The officer learned a lesson. He should have asked the soldier if he was feeling okay, at a minimum.

PT CADENCE

Soldiers who chat in PT formation are pulled out to call cadence. Their excess energy is used for the benefit of the entire formation.

Designate cadence callers before the run begins. There should always be a soldier designated to replace the one singing now. He or she does not have to *ask* to be relieved; his or her replacement watches for the signal to take over, never breaking cadence.

COMMAND EMPHASIS AT PT

The worse the weather, the more important for you to be there.

Attend physical training (PT) training with each of your sections and platoons. Command presence is important. This not only ensures that PT is tough, challenging and effective, it also demonstrates that you endure PT just as they do. Be aware that every eye will be (discreetly) on you. This is the time to show then that you give 100% as well as demanding it of them.

The absolute best time to join your subordinate leaders' PT formation is when the weather is the worst. If soldiers cannot see you enjoying grass drills on the frost-covered ground when they are, they assume you are sleeping in.

Real Life

One hundred twenty soldiers stood in formation, soaking wet. Thunder punched through the pouring rain, as lightning flashed and the ground dissolved into mud. The company commander, recognizing the hazards, canceled physical training.

As the captain sloshed into the building, he was confronted by the furious battalion executive officer, who spat the words, "Why did you cancel PT?

Only me and the battalion commander have that authority!"

The senior officer was absolutely correct. Coincidentally, he was too busy to participate in PT this frightful morning, as was the battalion commander.

OFFICER TRAINING RESPONSIBILITY

NCOs have an important role in an officer's development. Responsibility for officer training, however, remains with the officer's senior rater.

Effective training for officers also requires a defined goal, attainable intermediate objectives, and the personal involvement of the responsible senior officer. Do you have an officer training plan?

APPLYING YOUR PROFESSIONAL EDUCATION

How do you apply the formal professional education you received at NCO and officer professional education courses? These schools teach you the way things *ought* to be, according to the manuals. The people who make their living developing these courses may even think they are an accurate picture of what really happens. Do not believe it.

"The most important outcome of education is to become independent of formal education."

—PAUL E. GRAY IN
TECHNOLOGY REVIEW

Your unit and situation may not look anything like what you saw in school. You must take what you have and accomplish the mission. Talk to soldiers and supervisors. Get dirty. Take notes, ask questions; learn about your unit, your people, and your equipment. Only then can your formal education assist you. At a minimum, formal training sets a standard for operation of a weapon or other complex system, and is valuable for your training of others.

AFTER-ACTION REVIEW

"You can't expect to win if you don't know why you lose."

—BENJAMIN LIPSOM

It is not a beat-up session, nor an exchange of hugs and kisses. The more enjoyable it is, the less effective it is. Some attention is paid to what is going right; most of the precious time is dedicated to improving flaws.

The AAR facilitator is the key. His presentation is one-quarter subject matter expertise, 50% astute observations, and three-quarters theater. He will get you to say things you did not know you knew, to learn things you did not know you did not know.

SUPPLY CONFIDENCE

"Forget logistics and you lose."

—LT. GEN. F. M. FRANKS

A confident commander ensures that everything is signed for, including all the hidden excess in the supply room and the motor pool. Even more important, he or she ensures his or her unit has all the equipment and supplies needed to perform the unit's mission in combat.

REPORTS OF SURVEY

Weak soldiers who have lost or damaged equipment often feel they have nothing to lose and everything to gain by insisting on a report of survey.

Accepting personal responsibility is a sign of strong character.

Advise a soldier that if the survey finds him negligent he will face not only the financial cost but also punishment (UCMJ) for negligence, if appropriate. If he knows he is guilty, he may elect to do the honest thing immediately.

Real Life

The NCO ordered him to drive through the creek. The specialist reluctantly complied, and inched into the water, past the sign that clearly stated the water was too deep. As the two soldiers and their doomed Hummer approached the midpoint of the swollen creek, the current pushed them downstream, where the rocky bottom dropped into a deep hole. In a few seconds, the only indication of the Hummer was the tip of its antenna trailing above the swift water and two wet soldiers on the bank.

The battalion commander found the NCO guilty of negligence. The sergeant forfeited one month's pay for his mistake, although the damage to the vehicle was many times that amount. Soon afterward, the specialist who drove the ill-fated vehicle requested to speak to the battalion commander. The colonel agreed, expecting to hear an emotional plea to relieve the sergeant of responsibility.

The young soldier reported to the commander and stated, "Sir, my sergeant was wrong to try to cross the creek." The colonel's face showed his surprise, then he said, "You're right, so what's your point?" The specialist continued, "I knew better too, sir. I should receive the same punishment."

The astounded colonel explained that because of the high cost of the damages, deducting additional money from the young specialist would not affect the amount charged to the NCO. The soldier replied, "I know, sir. But it's something I have to do."

He lived the example of integrity, loyalty, and moral courage, a great young soldier.

INVENTORY

Schedule inventories in advance to allow preparation. On the appointed day and time the equipment is laid out in accordance with your instructions. Your supply sergeant should be on hand with blank statements-of-charges. Any shortages are paid for TODAY. If the hand receipt holder insists on a survey, you must initiate one TODAY.

During inventories, carefully account for all basic issue items (BII), additionally authorized items (AAI), and subcomponents. The technical manual or supply catalog is the only approved reference.

Conduct a monthly, random, 10% inventory in addition to the commander's required 10% inventory. Always keep the results on file.

When a supply sergeant or hand receipt holder changes, conduct a 100% inventory, immediately.

EQUIPMENT FIELD LOSS

The commander may write-off up to $100 at the end of a field problem. Do not use this to cover negligence. If the soldier was wrong, he pays for it.

KEY CONTROL

Who is responsible for key control in each section? Has key control been checked? Check the CSDP (Command Supply Discipline Program) checklist and the current key control regulation.

Key control is the most neglected responsibility in a unit. (Okay, automation security, AR 380-380, is actually the most neglected.)

HAND RECEIPTS

Losing property during peacetime will kill you. If you are tactically and technically ignorant you may still have a modest 20-year career. If you lose control of property accountability, you haven't a prayer.

Sub-hand receipt everything to the user level. Keep copies of your master hand re-

You keep the originals of your hand receipts and sub-hand receipts.

ceipt on file as well as your subordinates' sub-hand receipts. Make sure they balance. Personally, manually, re-check each time you sign your hand receipt. The computer is an aid, not the total answer. Do not rely solely on the computer.

Your hand receipts are irreplaceable. Safeguard them as you would a thousand-dollar bill. If they disappear or "lose" pages, you will face an embarrassing and expensive encounter with an angry battalion commander.

Review and re-sign hand receipts when the owner gets his evaluation report in addition to the regularly scheduled inventories.

CLOTHING INVENTORY
AKA The Cothing Show-down Inspection
Do the troops have their full basic issue? Doubtful. Insist the supply sergeant check your gear and other leaders' before inspecting your soldiers.

THE COMMANDER'S HAND RECEIPT
Assuming command is often called the most important day in an officer's career. The day he or she signs for the company property, and becomes legally responsible for millions of dollars' worth of equipment, is also a critical day. The happiest day is when the commander passes his hand receipt to his replacement.

The best time to prepare for your outgoing change-of-hand-receipt inventory is while conducting your incoming inventory. Insist on a technical manual, supply bulletin, or memorandum for record for every item you sign for. Items lacking a manual should be photographed.

The regulation requires that every item on the property book be on hand, on order with a valid document number, or be part of an ongoing report-of-survey investigation to assign responsibility for its loss. Cut corners here at your peril.

The battalion commander usually requires a periodic update on the status of the inventory. Ensure that he or she is immediately informed of problems. He or she will have to brief the brigade commander on embarrassing shortages or expensive losses.

PROSPERING PROFESSIONALLY

YOUR BOSS'S GOALS AND YOURS
Know the goals, objectives, and priorities of your boss. This comes from your copy of his or her Officer Evaluation Report Support Form, the quarterly training guidance (QTG), and above all, personal communication.

With you boss's goals in mind, set your own job description. Remember that you are valuable to your boss only because you make his or her commitments, programs, and priorities happen. If you stop making things happen, you stop being important.

SUPPORT OF YOUR BOSS
You gain nothing by publicly embarrassing your boss. When you allow your enthusiasm to overpower your judgment, you lose all your silver bullets. You demonstrate that you may be smart but you certainly are not wise.

> *"Avoid victories over superiors."*
> —ALTASAR GRACIAN Y MORALES

*"An officer . . . should
make it a cardinal
principle of life that no
act of commission or
omission on his part will
cause his immediate
superior to make a
mistake."*

—GENERAL MALIN CRAIG, USA:
ADDRESS TO THE GRADUATING
CLASS, WEST POINT, 12 JUNE 1937

*"Discipline must be
imposed, but loyalty
must be earned—yet
the highest form of
discipline exists only
when there is mutual
loyalty, up and down."*

—MAJOR GENERAL AUBREY "RED"
NEWMAN, *FOLLOW ME,* 1981

*General George S. Patton
said the same thing:
"There is a great deal of
talk about loyalty from
the bottom to the top;
loyalty from the top
down is even more
necessary and much less
prevalent."*

—GEORGE S. PATTON, JR.:
WAR AS I KNEW IT, 1947

DON'T HIDE BAD NEWS

Don't hide bad news; it does not get better with age. Bad news is far less painful if you bring a proposed solution with you at the presentation.

THE BOSS'S LOYALTY

Beware the boss who says he values integrity but really means loyalty—loyalty to him.

UNIT RECOVERY

If you cannot brief the recovery process in detail then you:

- Do not have a plan;
- Have a plan that you do not know well and cannot possibly supervise;
- Have not read the SOP.

Having a detailed recovery plan is only half the battle. If it is not followed, it is just another wasted page in the manual.

LEADERS' BRIEF

An informed leader should be able to brief, at least, the following to his boss at any time.

PERSONNEL:

- Number authorized vs. on hand.
- Near-term losses and status of their evaluation report & award nominations.
- Soldiers on Exceptional Family Member Program (EFMP).
- Single parents without a family care plan.

- Who is the next to act as an incoming sponsor.
- Physical fitness test failures.
- Overweight soldiers.
- Reenlistment eligible soldiers.
- Those barred from reenlistment.
- Recent incidents of indiscipline (drugs, speeding, arrest, etc.).
    TRAINING:
- Current assessment of METL task proficiency.
- Percentage of unit that passed the most recent PT test.
- Retraining plan for fitness test failures.
- Status of weapon qualification.
    TRAINING GUIDANCE:

Do you have a copy of the current commander's training guidance? Is it being followed? Is it a paper drill, or will it be an ass-chewing exercise at the end of the term for failure to comply?

SUPPLY: Who is the hand receipt holder for each section? What is the key equipment shortage for each section? When was the last inventory? When is the next?

SURVIVORSHIP BRIEFING

Present a mandatory class on the benefits of survivors of an active-duty death. The postcasualty services section will conduct the class or provide the material for unit leaders to present it.

Encourage each soldier to develop an emergency folder listing his or her insurance, and other important information. Casualty or retirement services will provide a recommended list.

Think of the worst officer or NCO you have ever known. Imagine that person serving as the casualty assistance officer for your loved ones in their time of greatest need. That is why you need this briefing.

"One of the advantages of being a captain is being able to ask for advice without necessarily having to take it."

—WILLIAM SHATNER AS KIRK, IN "DAGGER OF THE MIND"

ADVICE

While a senior leader may not have to take advice, a wise leader will ask for it, and consider it when the situation allows. Accepting input from subordinates doesn't make you weak. It makes your smart.

"Shallow men believe in luck . . . Strong men believe in cause and effect."

—RALPH WALDO EMERSON, *THE CONDUCT OF LIFE,* "WORSHIP", 1860

LUCK

With all due respect to Mr. Emerson, sometimes you are good at your job, sometimes you are lucky; either way it counts. In the long run, you should rely more on skill than luck.

YOUR BOSS'S OER SUPPORT FORM

Real Life

The company commanders each requested a copy of their support battalion commander's performance ob-

jectives. They got it. The official Army form and the attached continuation sheets detailed great expectations for the maintenance company's expensive repair parts inventory. It made no mention of the distribution or medical company missions.

What conclusion did the distribution and medical company commanders draw?

SILVER BULLETS

You must know when to fall on your sword over a soldier's predicament, or other issue. The use of such "silver bullets" is a limited and precious resource. Each one you use diminishes your ability to do that in the future.

You are effectively using some of your boss's personal respect for your opinion to change his mind. When you persuade him to change his mind, and you are right, you gain an extra bullet. If you are wrong you may be out of ammunition, out of respect, and out of a job.

On the other hand, if you and your boss always agree on everything, you are only an echo, not a leader.

What are the calamities that you should never try to mitigate with your silver bullets?

"You are effectively using up some of the respect your boss has for your opinion to change his mind."

—COL RONALD ROBINSON

Drug use and other moral or ethical failures should be at the top of the list. Keep in mind that your subordinates, peers, and seniors will grade you on who and what you fight for.

COMMITMENT TO SOLDIERS

You cannot simply tell soldiers you are committed to their welfare. You must demonstrate it. They hear what you say, they believe what they see.

Real Life

The twenty-mile march began in bitter cold, and ended in freezing rain and mud. The sodden column of weary soldiers marched directly to the dining hall, anticipating hot food and relief from the icy drizzle.

They arrived to find the doors locked. The cooks had prepared the meal but blocked the doors in order to protect their sparkling floors. Every eye was on the company commander as he approached the sergeant in charge of the mess hall, expecting an explosion of furious indignation at this cowardly and self-serving conduct.

As sweat slipped into chills, 190 exhausted soldiers sat on their wet rucksacks and shivered, eating hot dogs and succotash mixed with icy rain.

Their needless misery would soon be forgotten. Their newfound disappointment and distrust in their company commander would not.

How such a weak leader was placed in command of a company is yet another mystery.

DOCTRINE

Doctrine is theory. It is a clean, predictable, quantifiable, small gray area. Reality is a dirty, confusing, conflicting, ambiguous, large gray area.

Following doctrine is never an excuse for failure.

Schools grade you on your knowledge of doctrine; your boss grades you on results. Don't confuse the two grading scales.

But don't forget doctrine, either. You can't be a total freelancer. The purpose of doctrine—the army's way of conducting operations—is to prevent chaos in the battlefield, which is the ultimate place you want results.

END OF THE DUTY DAY

A boss who works 19 hours a day at the expense of his or her own family certainly doesn't care about your family. If you do not know when the end of the day is, how will your subordinates? Your must balance the

"There are no office hours for leaders."
—CARDINAL JAMES GIBBONS

needs of mission and soldiers. How well you balance that is constantly graded by your boss, and your soldiers.

VICTIM OF YOUR EXPERIENCE

"If the only tool in your toolbox is a hammer, every problem looks like a nail."

What we are often depends on what we have been. Current decisions are built on past experience. We are all victims of our experiences.

The most dangerous example is the leader whose early successes were the result of demanding huge sacrifices from subordinates and brutally punished dissent. He has learned that he is graded on paper results regardless of despicable personal leadership, and the broken and distrustful soldiers he has created and left behind will not be counted against him.

MISSION PRIORITY

"Never let the mission go down the drain simply for the sake of practicing good leadership."

—KENNETH BLANCHARD, THE ONE MINUTE MANAGER

The triad: my mission, my soldiers, myself. What has priority?

Answer: It depends.

It depends on the constraints of the mission and the condition of your soldiers and yourself. Obviously some missions are more important than the lives or well-being of anyone. That is rare.

You must balance the three.

What Has Priority

- If your soldiers are unable to continue the mission, what good are they?
- If you have been awake for 36 hours and expect to face critical decisions soon, perhaps the priority is for you to get some rest.

PERCEPTION: THE FIRST REPORT IS ALWAYS WRONG

A highly successful field grade officer often said: " . . . the first report is always wrong." He was usually right. How does this affect your ability to make decisions quickly, based on reports of your subordinates?

"In battle nothing is ever as good or as bad as the first reports of excited men would have it."

—FIELD MARSHAL SIR WILLIAM SLIM, *UNOFFICIAL HISTORY,* 1959

PLANNING EFFECTIVENESS

There are two kinds of people, those who make long-range plans . . . and those who work for those who make long-range plans. Anticipation determines what you need. Coordination gets what you need. Synchronization gets it at the right place and time.

"The main thing is to have a plan; if it is not the best plan, it is better than having no plan at all."

—GEN. JOHN MONASH, LETTER, 1918.

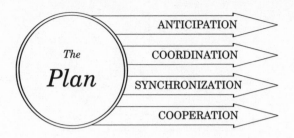

Cooperation is the magic grease that overcomes the friction of the battlefield. No plan is complete. Without cooperation (looking out for the other guys' success), unforeseen challenges will destroy the plan.

OPTIONAL SOCIAL FUNCTIONS

The function fly-by

Most social functions are enjoyable, but be careful of those that are advertised as optional; most are not. You are "strongly encouraged" to attend. You attend to support your boss, so make contact with him and others to ensure that you are seen. This is the function fly-by.

UNIT HAILS AND FAREWELLS

"The real art of conversation is not only to say the right thing in the right place, but to leave unsaid the wrong thing at the tempting moment."

—DOROTHY NEVILL

This is not the time to unburden your soul or settle old scores. No one invited you to hear a stinging rebuke or your scathing assessment of others' personal worth. Even if you feel wronged, you must not pour oil on trouble waters to the extent you can without gagging.

Real Life

The lieutenant recalled his company commander with great bitterness as he drank another beer at his final hail and farewell. He recounted the many instances of the commander's weakness and poor leadership, and the battalion commander's seeming indifference. As he spoke the small circle of fellow lieutenants nodded in agreement, for lieutenants are the harshest critics of captains.

"I'm going to tell it like it is," declared the tipsy young officer. "I'm gonna tell that worthless [deleted] captain what I really think of him," he said, sipping his beer. At that moment, the battalion commander called the younger officer to the podium while he delivered a stirring tribute to the young lieutenant and heartfelt regret at his departure. He then handed the microphone to the angry young man for his remarks. Every eye was on him, anticipating the fireworks. He paused before speaking, struggling at the crossroads of short-term gratification and professionalism, when his good sense and discipline finally overcome anger and alcohol. He smiled, and said only, "Good-bye."

After the party, the battalion commander approached the departing officer. They clasped hands for a moment, the colonel looked him in the eye and said, "Thanks." The lieutenant said nothing, but his eyes betrayed his disappointment, and his face displayed contempt.

STAFF

"There is nothing more dangerous than a sailor with a rifle except a young, inexperienced staff officer with a pencil."

—MG AUBREY "RED" NEWMAN

"The power of a good staff officer lies more in his feet than his pen," said a highly successful brigade level commander who, although not a staff officer, certainly practiced what he preached. He saw more and knew more than most of his staff and all of his chairbound peers.

DON'T LOSE YOUR SENSE OF HUMOR

Real Life

The battalion picnic included a raffle in which a young soldier won "Battalion Commander for a Day." The real battalion commander brought the lucky young man to the podium and asked what his first order would be. He replied to the waiting crowd, "Officer physical fitness test, 0600 tomorrow."

The only people not laughing were the officers.

TEN RULES TO LIVE BY × 3

NCO VS. SERGEANT
1. All units have too many sergeants and too few NCOs.
2. Sergeants depend on outside motivation; NCOs provide their own.
3. Sergeants enforce standards on others, but not themselves; NCOs live the standards and lead by example.
4. Sergeants crave attention; NCOs seek effectiveness.
5. Sergeants cover their asses; NCOs do the right thing, regardless of consequences.
6. Sergeants do what they have to do; NCOs do what needs to be done.
7. Sergeants are short-timers from their first day in the unit.
8. NCOs always leave their unit better than they found it.
9. Sergeants avoid responsibility; NCOs feel responsible for everything.
10. Sergeants are not respected, even by people who like them; NCOs are respected, even by those who do not like them.

SOLDIERS

1. Soldiers grade everything you do and say, or fail to do and say.
2. You are graded by their standards—not yours, and not your senior rater's.
3. When you think soldiers are not watching, they are.
4. If you think soldiers will never know what happens behind your office door, you are wrong.
5. They don't want you to be like them. They want you to understand them.
6. They hear what you say. They believe what they see.
7. They respect strength, when combined with integrity and competence, even in someone they don't like.
8. They despise weakness, even in someone they like.
9. Self-confidence is the first step to gaining their confidence.
10. Tales of your successes will grow over beer in the barracks. So will your failures.

LEADERSHIP
1. Be at the critical time and place—every day has (at least) one.
2. Everything in life is a graded event.
3. Common sense counts.
4. Discipline begins with self-discipline.
5. Wear your heart on your sleeve; your soldiers must know how you feel.
6. Subordinates learn by your example, whether you intend it or not.
7. Five minutes' checking on the guards in a freezing rain at midnight is worth a year of payday speeches.
8. Considering input doesn't make you weak; it makes you smart.
9. You gain authority by giving it.
10. What you see is as important as what you choose not to see.

THE SOLDIER'S CREED

I am an American soldier.

I am a warrior and a member of a team. I serve the people of the United States and live the Army values.

I will always place the mission first.

I will never accept defeat.

I will never quit.

I will never leave a fallen comrade.

I am disciplined, physically and mentally tough, trained and proficient in warrior tasks and drills. I always maintain my arms, my equipment, and myself.

I am an expert and a professional.

I stand ready to deploy, engage, and destroy the enemies of the United States of America in close combat.

I am a guardian of freedom and the American way of life.

Index